THE LEARNING
COACH APPROACH

To Jim,
With love and gratitude
for being there in the 11ᵗʰ hour—and A.B.

THE LEARNING COACH APPROACH

Inspire, Encourage, and Guide
Your Child Toward Greater
Success in School and in Life

By Linda Dobson

RUNNING PRESS
PHILADELPHIA · LONDON

9   8   7   6   5   4   3   2   1
Digit on the right indicates the number of this printing

Library of Congress Control Number: 2005922805

ISBN 13:978-0-7624-2400-9

ISBN 0-7624-2400-1

Top left and middle rightcover photo: © RubberBall/PictureQuest

Top right cover photo: © Index Stock Imagery/PictureQuest

Bottom left cover photo: © Stockdisc/PictureQuest

Cover and interior design by Amanda Richmond

Edited by Jennifer Kasius

This book may be ordered by mail from the publisher.
Please include $2.50 for postage and handling.
But try your bookstore first!

Running Press Book Publishers
125 South Twenty-second Street
Philadelphia, Pennsylvania 19103-4399

Visit us on the web!
www.runningpress.com

TABLE OF CONTENTS

INTRODUCTION

This book—and the learning coach approach—is for every parent who has watched a child she loves face a situation similar to the one the eldest of my three children was in. As he grew from infancy to school-age, my son was the most easygoing, laid back child I'd ever known. Accompanied by the typical oohs and aahs of reaching a cultural landmark, in 1984 he began attending half-day kindergarten. After six months of his beginning his day by stepping on to a yellow bus, I could no longer deny that he was changing for the worse. Despite my concerns his teacher repeatedly reassured me he was doing fine academically. Despite my questions the little six year-old couldn't articulate what might be causing the happy-go-lucky boy to slide into unhappiness, stomachaches, and disrespectful treatment of the baby sister he once adored. As it turned out, both in the classroom and with the bully on the bus ride home, my son was overburdened, agitated, and anxious, succumbing to physical and emotional stress increasingly affecting his health and well-being. Something had to change.

I checked into the only alternatives available—a couple of local private schools—but realized that such was merely a costly way of rearranging the deck chairs; it might help the situation *appear* different, but it would do nothing to fundamentally change the situation and so wouldn't stop the ship from sinking. When I was at my wit's end, I happened to turn on the TV at an unusual time. There was Phil Donahue, promising to be right back so that his lone guest, a veteran school teacher by the name of John Holt, could answer more questions about his newsletter, "Growing Without Schooling." Does that mean what I think it does? I wondered.

Indeed, John, a man I soon came to know and admire as the granddaddy of homeschooling, was talking about the small but growing number of parents who were choosing, for a wide variety of reasons, to teach their children at home themselves. It sounded like the answer—the only answer—to the problems my son was experiencing.

That day my family became "homeschoolers," foregoing my son's school attendance to rid his growing nervous system of stress. Yet because it was the only model I knew, I began our homeschooling journey by recreating school at home. Thus began a long and sometimes painful process to get to a pivotal truth that first transformed learning for our family, then ultimately for readers of my books. By eventually eliminating school and its methods from our lives, by taking responsibility for the education of the few children I loved dearly right along with the responsibility for their care and feeding, learning was no longer segregated from life, but an integral part of it.

This allowed me to stop thinking in terms of teaching, and something wonderful happened. By focusing on learning, I created the time to do something more important than teaching, more important to achieve the elusive goal of fun, easy, and effective learning—this was simply to *observe* the children for the vast majority of information I needed to guide them. I applied this knowledge daily to keep individual curiosity stoked, to connect today's lessons to the promise of independent life tomorrow.

This knowledge was the seed of what almost twenty years later I call "the learning coach approach." After many years of reading, researching, writing, observing, studying, thinking, and interviewing countless homeschooling parents and children, I've boiled down this by-product of the homeschooling boom into one guiding sentence.

Curiosity creates interest, interest increases attention to the task at hand, and attention gives rise to learning.

Here is the first of a variety of Coach's Motivational Minutes you will find tucked into the upcoming pages.

COACH'S MOTIVATIONAL MINUTE: Print out this sentence on large type on your computer: Curiosity creates interest, interest increases attention to the task at hand, and attention gives rise to learning. Keep it where you can see it every day, on the refrigerator or even better, on the bathroom wall.

My pet name for this adage is "seal," spelled C-I-A-L, for curiosity, interest, attention, learning. To further help you remember it, C-I-A-L, as at the end of *special*. The learning coach approach is about saying *yes* to your child's curiosity and interests in a way only a parent can. With the burgeoning research on learning and the functions of the brain, what may be the single biggest fatal flaw in the institutional approach to education is revealed.

No matter how much rhetoric about educational excellence that politicians contribute, no matter how many calls for better pay and more respect for teachers that the unions demand, no matter how innovative the latest curriculum on CD or on-line, and *even* no matter how deeply taxpayers reach into their pockets to pay for it all, the underlying curiosity that propels the learning process simply cannot be accommodated in a classroom setting where one or even a few adults are paid to "teach" twenty to thirty children.

I feel very fortunate that my experience with my children showed me there is a fundamental difference between teaching and coaching learning. My dictionary defines "to teach" as "to impart knowledge or skill to; give instruction to." By virtue of this definition, the learner is merely a passive recipient of actions by the teacher.

On the other hand, a parent who makes education a household priority can become a coach who instead "facilitates" learning, which means "to free from difficulties or obstacles; make easier; aid; assist." By virtue of *this* definition, the learner moves front and center. No longer a mere passive recipient, your child becomes an active creator of his education. Passive recipients of information burn out; active creators of education get fired up.

When I began exploring the phenomenon of coaching sweeping the country, I saw many similarities between what I know home-schooling parents routinely do and the advice coaches give to business professionals. Both work to inspire students/employees toward greater potential, increased productivity, and deeper commitment. Both accentuate the personal values and habits necessary to achieve the happiness, peace, balance, and prosperity we all wish for in great abundance in our children's lives. Yet despite all the similarities between coaching (facilitating) and learning at home, no one has applied the principles of the coaching formula to learning, let alone made them accessible to the millions of parents who perhaps like you want to help their children succeed in school yet don't feel they possess the tools to do so.

As a homeschooling "veteran," the last twenty years of my life's work have been devoted to helping parents incorporate the above-mentioned benefits into just as many children's lives as possible. However, I wasn't reaching the vast majority of parents—those whose children attend school. That's why I was so excited to gather together the simple and fun secrets that homeschooling parents have discovered about helping children learn at home and put them between the covers of *What the Rest of Us Can Learn from Homeschooling*. Today I'm even more enthusiastic about sharing the simplified way any parent can help guide her child to increased academic success by becoming a "learning coach."

Don't bother yourself with ideas of needing to become yet another teacher in your child's life. Start thinking in terms of freeing your child from learning difficulties and obstacles. The perspective will be a lot more fun—and successful—for both of you.

As it turns out, the vast majority of learning isn't about teaching at all. It happens morning, noon, and night every single day one is alive and conscious. It's as natural —and imperceptible—as breathing. When it comes to learning, less is more. Less pressure, more fun. Less scheduling, more free time. Success, in its many forms, results not by pushing children into activities but by creating an environment that encourages exploration and discovery, and supporting their curiosity. As one of the people who most loves your child, you can and will make all the difference in the world by integrating learning into your daily lives together. Welcome to the world of the parent learning coach.

CHAPTER 1:

THE LEARNING COACH APPROACH

Just as she has for 180 days each year for a little over a decade, Mary enters her eighth grade classroom at least half an hour before the children arrive. While the room is still peaceful she plans to organize supplies for a morning science project and make sure she has all the necessary permission slips for an upcoming field trip. But next week's "high stakes" state achievement tests move from their ever-present seat at the back of her mind to the front. She sighs as she tries to make herself comfortable behind her wooden desk and pulls in front of her a stack of her students' most recent writing assignments.

Anna's paper is on top, illegible as always. Jason's and Zoe's are as good as expected, but then there's Ryan's. At first glance it appears "the" and "a" are the only two words spelled right in the entire paragraph. He got off the subject in his second sentence and never returned. And Erik's. Poor, sweet Erik could churn out a complete story each hour, but his hands just can't keep up with his vivid imagination.

"Just like last year's horrifying statistics, that's four out of six in this classroom unlikely to pass the writing portion of the test," Mary says out loud while placing Erik's paper on the bottom of the pile. "Now there's talk about making these test scores a full twenty-five percent of the children's fourth quarter report card grades so preparing for it takes up all of our time. If I could spend just ten minutes one-on-one with these children every day—*just ten minutes*—I know it would make a world of difference in their understanding. I could present the material to each one in a way that makes sense, not for a test, but for *the individual*." Mary sighs again.

Mary sighs because she knows all too well the tale of the test. In June 2003, the National Assessment of Educational Progress (the Nation's Report Card), reported that 36 percent of 4th graders cannot read at what the test defined as a "basic" level. Not only are scores equally dismal in other basic subjects, the evidence strongly suggests the situation gets worse, not better, as these children reach high school.

One of the reasons may be the potpourri of negative learning labels slapped on children today. Eager to proactively help their children, parents buy and read the myriad books specializing in one label or another, only to be told how to make the best of the situation. Yet while no education theorists have convincingly explained *why* we're producing so many "learning disabled" children all of a sudden (and, interestingly, the United States is the only country producing them in near-epidemic proportion), current research on learning, coupled with the undeniably faltering state of public education, points toward a situation that might be more accurately described as "teaching disabled."

Despite the necessity of a school's singular approach to teaching, mounting evidence leaves little doubt that *all children don't learn in the same way*. The traditional classroom situation is often inadequate to properly address the unique learning needs of individual children. Throw in a small tidbit that anyone who has ever observed two children for even an hour picks up—*all children are not interested in the same things at the same time*—and you're on to the recipe that is creating a learning crisis in the classroom.

In addition, many parents are beginning to see that in a classroom filled with twenty to thirty children, their child receives an equivalent fraction of attention. (A recent University of California Los Angeles project reveals the average schooled student receives seven minutes of personal attention for each day spent in the classroom.) When a classroom contains children with special needs or behavior problems, the percentage of attention for the majority of children dwindles further. How could it be any other way?

Now for good measure throw in President Bush's No Child Left Behind Act, known as NCLB for short. (At the federal government's Web site, www.ed.gov/nclb, you can find an overview of the Act.) While proponents and opponents debate whether or not the Act helps the theoretical intention of boosting public school quality, it's hard to deny NCLB's accountability measures add yet another layer to an already bloated bureaucracy. It's also creating a lot of confusion among parents.

WHAT DOES "NO CHILD
LEFT BEHIND" MEAN, EXACTLY?

President George W. Bush signed the No Child Left Behind Act in January 2002, making it the law of the land. In the proposed 2005 budget, a share of a whopping $38.7 billion, or 8.2 percent of total public K-12 education funding (the highest percentage of federal funding in history), is at stake. Any school wanting its share of the money must dance to the tune of the piper, and the vast majority does.

In exchange for the funds, NCLB expanded testing programs and set forth the penalties if and when enough students fail to meet math and reading standards. Not only could a school lose cold, hard cash it has counted on, it can suffer the humiliation of appearing on a "failing schools" list. A school that appears on such a list for two years in a row must give parents the option of transferring their children to another school.

Part of the parental confusion develops because each state has also created its own rating system and, inevitably, there are discrepancies between its evaluation and that of the federal government's. In North Carolina, for example, more than thirty-two schools considered excellent by the state failed the federal test for progress. The feds considered 317 California schools low performing even as they exhibited exemplary academic growth on the state's performance index. The feds called seventy-five percent of Florida's "high-performing" schools "low-performing." More schools in some states, like Georgia, Delaware, and Kentucky, met the federal goals. More schools in other states, such as Iowa, Oregon, and Minnesota, were placed on academic probation.

Conflicting report cards aside, parents are misinterpreting the very essence of No Child Left Behind. During the back-to-school season in 2004, the *Hartford* (Connecticut) *Courant* came right out and asked parents of school-aged children what NCLB was all about.

One thought it meant children shouldn't be left alone after school. Another believed NCLB prohibited leaving children alone on the street. Still other parents guessed it meant that a school couldn't hold a child back in a grade, even if that child failed. Indeed, a 2004 Phi Delta Kappa/Gallup Poll revealed that 62 percent of parents of public school children said they knew "very little or nothing at all" about the law that is increasingly driving both educators' actions and events in the classroom.

We will soon explore being an informed education consumer in more depth. But if you have children in school, start researching NCLB and its impact on your child's school and your child right now. It will help you understand how unseen forces affect daily classroom activity.

IS YOUR CHILD FIRED UP—
OR BURNED OUT—ON LEARNING?

I can't say why, when, or how it happened, but it did. At some point after compulsory schooling began a mere 150 years or so ago, our society accepted it as perfectly normal and natural: Children hate going to school. As if this wasn't bad enough, the school culture itself enforces the notion with an unwritten rule that those who are smart and/or enjoy classes are geeks, nerds, or just plain weird.

Then there's that compulsion feature itself, compounded by NCLB's focus on test scores. How often does the situation in

Jennifer's home play out across the nation?

"Three years ago Bethany couldn't wait to go to kindergarten," Jennifer remembers, "and she thrived. But within the first few months of first grade her attitude began to change. At first she just complained that she had to go to school, but by third grade she actively fought it." Exasperated, Jennifer was unsuccessful trying to talk with Bethany, so she turned to the teacher.

"It happens all the time," the teacher told Jennifer. "She's burned out."

"How does an eight-year-old 'burn out'?" Jennifer asked.

"There are a variety of contributing factors," the teacher confided. "For some kids, we move too quickly and they can't keep up. For others, the opposite is true; they get bored and tune out. Some don't really wake up until after they've been in school for hours, while others get distracted while trying to keep childhood energy in check enough to sit still. Some don't see a purpose, and still others just plain aren't interested in what I'm talking about. Try as we might, it's impossible to be all things to all children, and we lose some along the way. For what it's worth," the teacher added, "Bethany is extremely bright and creative. That's how we lost her."

"Lost her?" exclaims Jennifer. "My baby still had months to go in this woman's classroom and she considered her 'lost'? I don't think I've ever been so angry in my life, and I vowed then and there to change burned out on learning to fired up at home."

So what did Jennifer do when she didn't want to lose any more precious family time together to school-related activities? *Especially* when she was unable to take complete educational responsibility through homeschooling?

In the warmth and comfort of home, she became Bethany's learning coach. Instead of acting as just another in a long string of teachers, drilling the multiplication tables or quizzing her child on a long list of dates related to the Revolutionary War, Jennifer focused on three elements vital to academic success that aren't addressed in crowded (or even many uncrowded) classrooms.

- One-on-one attention
- Basic learning skills the child may apply to any area of study
- Educational customization based on learning style, innate intelligences, and interests

Researchers, too, are noticing the results of facilitating learning in lieu of teaching. In 2002, the University of North Florida's Rebecca A. Marcon reported on a comparison between three diverse preschool models. The first was child-initiated, including lots of free exploration of interests. Next was the academically directed approach, focusing on early curriculum material. The third was a "combination" approach. Marcon writes, "By the end of their sixth year in school, children whose preschool experiences had been academically directed earned significantly lower grades compared to children who had attended child-initiated preschool classes. Children's later school success appears to have been enhanced by more active, child-initiated early learning experiences."

Light Your Child's Learning Fire with His Interests

While this study focuses on one specific group of young children, the results support the experiences of learning coach families across all social, economic, political, and religious spectra and with all ages of children. Think about it for a minute. Did you do better in school in those subjects you liked, or disliked? Children—young and old—learn best when they're *interested*. While the teachers in school must follow the same old program, you as coach can take the easier, faster route of discovering, then using that which best motivates your child to learn—his interests. Through these you will guide, inspire, encourage, and integrate learning into everyday life.

Elizabeth, a registered nurse, knew her younger son, Matthew, would quickly get lost as his class marched forward through their math textbook if he didn't grasp the multiplication concept soon. "Matthew loves anything dinosaur," Elizabeth explains, "so we took the largest piece of heavy cardboard I could find and created a stand-up 'dinosaur habitat' on it. It has everything—trees, caves, even a tar pit. But all around it also has "real" nests for dinosaur eggs made from construction paper."

As mother and son enjoyed playing with the habitat one day, Elizabeth threw two eggs in each of the ten nests, then asked Matthew how many new baby dinosaurs were on the way. She sat patiently as Matthew counted each and every one. "I know a short-cut that will have you knowing how many dinosaur babies there will be even quicker," Elizabeth told Matthew. "We have ten nests, right? So we'll count by two's ten times."

After a couple of run-throughs, Matthew said, "So every time you have two, ten times, it's twenty?"

"The light bulb turned on!" Elizabeth remembers. "The next night after dinner he couldn't wait to get back to the habitat after I put a different number of eggs in different numbers of nests, four eggs each in six baskets, seven eggs each in nine baskets, and so on.

Matthew is 'hooked' on multiplication, and his math test scores reflect it."

Capitalizing on children's interests is one major way in which coaching differs from the traditional idea of teaching. There are five additional important differences.

A different relationship

The nature of the school system is such that teachers and administrators must maintain a hierarchical relationship with students. They become the "authority" to which students are held accountable and to whose standards they must aspire. A learning coach becomes a partner in the learning process, creating a relationship with your child much more conducive to cooperation, respect, and understanding.

A different way of dispensing what your child needs to know

In order to track progress, a step essential to the traditional school approach, information is provided to children in a predetermined sequence so all children may be tested on their "receipt" of the information in the same way at the same time.

As a learning coach, you can give your child the pleasure of discovery, an element vital to enjoying the learning process. You need not merely dispense information. You are free to help your child explore and discover the information he *wants*, the other half of enjoying the learning process.

A different guiding agenda

We would never demand that *all* children play baseball every day, because common sense tells us that not everyone will be good at or enjoy the game. Yet we have prescribed what we believe every child should study every day at the same time, and it became the course your child's school chose for her. It's called the curriculum, a name derived from a Latin root that means "a running." The curriculum guides the teaching agenda in schools, and it doesn't matter how fast or slow, good or bad, your child happens to be "running," he is on the same course as everyone else, one with a "finish line" that becomes the main goal.

Not so at home. Through the learning coach's freedom to customize a learning agenda, your child's course may become as simple or complicated as desired, lead anywhere you'd both like, and contains the countless "side trips" that a true discovery learning process may require. Best of all, you'll see that a "finish line" is only an illusion, as you'll both recognize learning as a lifelong process that adds meaning and value to every life activity.

A different way to assess progress

Whether we liked it or not, most of us spent our formative years having our academic prowess measured in relation to the prowess of others and held up to something called "a norm," an average of what all the other little children in the same grade were able to accomplish. As if that anonymous "norm" weren't enough, we sat in class and compared test grades, and rapidly decided which was the best and worst reading group based on who was assigned to each.

Some of us knew we'd never reach that "norm" in math or English, science or foreign language. Or, after enough failed attempts, we stopped spinning our wheels and trying. Others, quite aware of how easily they could exceed that norm, stopped taking much of it seriously. Along with the others at all the points in-between, as children we allowed that norm and the performance of others to dictate our sense of how smart—or dumb—we were.

The truth is that learning is a very personal act entered into by folks with varying degrees of ability, interest, and determination. Your child's starting point is not the same as the child's next door. If the same two children entered a two mile race and one started even just a few yards ahead of the other, would we determine how well they ran by comparing their finish times? Of course not, yet this is exactly what happens every day in classrooms across the country.

As your child's learning coach you can move progress assessment back where it belongs—to success measured through personal growth. One year, Brad and Michelle knew their only child, Brad, Jr., was way behind his classmates in understanding division, so they incorporated "division lessons" into everything from putting toys on shelves to divvying up food at the table. "Brad, Jr. was led to believe he wasn't 'normal,' and his classmates were merciless when he couldn't come up with answers when requested in class," says Brad. "His resultant lack of confidence was beginning to manifest as a loss of interest in learning."

Then came the wonderful day Brad, Jr. *did* unlock the mystery of division. "He was so proud," Michelle remembers, "so I took advantage of that. I explained it doesn't matter if it took him a little longer than his buddies; that the most important thing was that he kept working at it until he succeeded. While at this point no one at school cared one way or another that he understood, he still benefited from the sense of accomplishment he deserved because we, his parents, were paying attention."

It's easy to see which approach more readily serves to inspire a child toward future progress.

A remarkably different outcome

Wait for the teacher to tell you what to read. Wait for the teacher to tell you which questions to answer. Wait for the teacher to say you may start and must stop. Wait for the teacher to tell you what to study. The teacher has all the answers. Such an approach encourages the learner to become dependent upon another for much of the responsibility for her own education. It's hard to imagine we could create any larger roadblocks on the path to responsible independence for young adults than this.

It's easy to clear away that roadblock by coaching for autonomy. Learning coaches encourage educational independence by aiding the learning process, not by doing all the thinking for the child. This puts your child on a clear path toward being able to find answers for herself, and a self-directed student is a wonder to behold.

DO YOU BELIEVE IN GENIUS?

Many parents of the approximately 47 million school-aged children in America today have long assumed that everything educationally necessary was occurring in the classroom. Many also dream their children will grow as "geniuses," ultimately contributing something wonderful and useful to society. At the same time, we know that putting a child on the educational fast track—with too much pressure and exaggerated expectations—can make an otherwise enjoyable educational experience a nightmare for the would-be geniuses.

According to a 1960 study called "The Childhood Pattern of Genius" by Harold McCurdy, then a University of North Carolina professor of psychology, and published by the Smithsonian Institute, the route to genius may just be a much kinder, gentler track than many imagine.

After intensive study of the biographies of twenty geniuses, McCurdy noticed three aspects common to their lives during the typical development pattern as children.

- "A high degree of attention focused on the child by parents and other adults, expressed in intensive educational measures and usually, abundant love."
- "Isolation from other children, especially outside the family."
- "A rich efflorscence of fantasy [i.e., creativity] as a reaction to the preceding conditions."

But wait—there's more. McCurdy concluded, "It might be remarked that the mass education of our public school system is, in its way, a vast experiment on the effect of reducing all three factors to a minimum; accordingly, it should tend to suppress the occurrence of genius."

This conclusion should scare the hell out of every American citizen. But for parents, it should serve as a clarion call as to the utter importance of providing, not more schooling, but something very *different*. Let it shed light on the reality that not only *can* every parent become a child's learning coach, it's imperative that every parent does so.

COACHING: A PERFECT FIT FOR TWENTY-FIRST CENTURY EDUCATION

Plummeting test scores, school terror and violence, an increase in the number of children complaining of stress and depression, and observation of basic skills that don't measure up to report card grades have all played a role in the booming awareness of and need for educational alternatives. But nothing has impacted the shape and delivery of those alternatives as has twenty-first century technology—computers and the Internet—available for increasingly affordable prices to American families.

Where once the school building was known as the information "storehouse," today the Internet serves as a collection of global information on any matter of interest or need. The same information typically dispensed in schools, in the same curriculum format, can be found on the Internet. But the Internet has also thrown open a door to information you and your child can take at will, 365 days each year, in any order or sized chunk you care to digest.

Availability of information and the ability to freely choose how it is received are the emerging hallmarks of twenty-first century education. Taking advantage of these hallmarks represents a drastic departure from even your own educational experience just one generation ago.

Sadly, school systems mired in the status quo and providing a large percentage of employment in every metropolitan city and rural town show little interest in changing. But who can blame them? Freeing individual children and families to assume some degree of educational responsibility would rapidly reveal the status quo as an antiquated, inefficient, totally-dispensable-in-the-21st-century system. Promoting the availability, ease, speed, and customization available today—right now—to anyone who wishes to partake, would surely hasten what many already see as the system's inevitable demise.

"I really struggled through science in school—and summer school," remembers Sally, a real estate agent with three children. "It must be in the genes, because recently my daughter, Alicia, was suffering the same fate. I tried to help with her homework, but it didn't work. Then one night, after I felt like the worst mother on the planet for yelling, 'Alicia, I can't believe you don't understand this—this is the *easy* part,' I knew I had to do *something* different."

On a whim, Sally booted up her computer that night and after surfing until 1 AM "hadn't even scratched the surface of available help!" After school the next day she greeted Alicia at the door with two pages of Internet addresses offering everything from alternative texts to "instant homework help" to interactive, home-friendly experiments. "Her favorite seems to be www.sciencemadesimple. com," says Sally, where she enjoys the projects and almost always finds one related to whatever they're studying in class, and has taken to watching science in the news at the site, too. "What a relief to know I can best help Alicia, not by pushing her through a textbook she doesn't understand, but by keeping my eyes and ears open for *different* ways to accomplish the same thing. And neither one of us misses that fighting!"

Tom, a single dad to Nathan, took another route in their home. "I could tell Nathan really enjoyed writing science fiction, but I couldn't do much more than read what he wrote and comment, 'Yes, this is very good,'" says Tom.

Tom knew a co-worker was getting lots of good advice via an email group of professional financial planners, so he wondered if a similar group existed for science fiction writers. "My buddy's group was on yahoolists.com, so I checked," Tom says. "Sure enough, there were a couple of groups that looked good for Nathan. Now I still encourage him, of course, but he gets *real* advice and constructive criticism on a couple of lists with people who share his passion."

Countless other families also daily discover the helpful educational resources available via the computers sitting in their living rooms and dens. But this is only a brief, first glimpse at the opportunities that await parents willing to embrace the emerging possibilities of twenty-first century education. Let it help you boldly step out of the role of homework enforcer into the much more pleasant role of learning coach.

CHAPTER 2

THE LEARNING COACH
JOB DESCRIPTION

The learning coach approach is an easy and fun, middle ground between the total educational responsibility of homeschooling and merely making sure homework gets done. It provides the opportunity for you and your child to become a learning team, working together in the comfort of your home learning gym.

You do not, I repeat, you do *not* need a teacher's degree, nor in-depth knowledge of educational theory, nor twenty years of experience on a school board or as PTA or PTO president.

In fact, many experienced learning coaches will tell you that any amount of this type of background often makes it more *difficult* for you to act as your child's coach, so different are teaching and coaching.

You will find you already have everything you need to be an effective learning coach by virtue of being one of the people who loves your child, and knowing her better than anyone else in the world.

Your knowledge of the unique individual that is your child will allow you to guide, inspire, encourage, and integrate learning into your everyday lives until your child has become an independent, responsible adult, at which time you've worked your way out of a job!

If a learning coach job description was to appear in your local paper, it might read something like this:

WANTED: Open hearted parent who enjoys and appreciates her child, or would at least give it a good shot. Brief training in learning styles and multiple intelligences required, in preparation for greater amounts of time spent observing child for evidence of these, as well as to discover what lights her learning fire. Ability to create and maintain home as learning gym essential. Must be open-minded enough to build a learning lifestyle, yet humble enough to guide instead of lead. Benefits include but are not limited to stronger family ties and use of the entire world as your child's classroom.

Can you do the job? You bet you can! Begin by saying *yes* to your child's curiosity and giving C-I-A-L the time, resources, and guidance to develop. I know it doesn't sound much like what you remember from your school experience. I know it flies in the face of the way professional educators attempt to teach millions of children every day. But you will be pleasantly surprised to discover that the differences in the learning coach approach teem with potential for your child.

DON'T FOCUS ON THE LEARNING

One of the most surprising discoveries for new learning coaches is how much children learn when the adults don't focus on the learning! In this way there are a lot more time and space for natural curiosity, and for creating interest that increases attention to the task at hand. You'll find that attention gives rise to learning.

Jessie, six year-old Gary's learning coach, noticed how her son would run to the maps on his bedroom walls, or to the large world map posted in the laundry room, whenever he learned about a new place. "He practically lives for that," Jessie says. "All of his subjects can revolve around that. For example," Jessie continues, "Switzerland was our topic one week when he was learning how to tell time in math. All I had to do was tell him it was a different time there than it was here, and he quickly mastered the clock so he could figure out what time it was there. He was studying American holidays so we looked up what holidays are celebrated in Switzerland and noted the similarities and differences. The teacher was establishing sight vocabulary so I made a rough map and labeled it with words like map, Alps, mountains, watches, chocolate. Gary *wanted* to learn the words, and was more than happy to practice the alphabetizing he needed to know with them."

COACH'S MOTIVATIONAL MINUTE: Don't automatically equate a child being put through the paces of a lesson with a child who is actually learning something. In many instances, real learning that "sticks," as opposed to learning that is lost after the test is over, is a by-product of an interesting experience, and the opportunity to connect something new with what is already known. The most effective learning is often incidental to the experience, and not the experience's primary purpose. "The brain," wrote Pat Wolfe and Ron Brandt in a 1998 Educational Leadership article titled "What Do We Know from Brain Research?" "is essentially curious and it must be to survive. It constantly seeks connections between the new and the known." Start with curiosity and interest, and watch learning grow.

EVERY PARENT IS A PERFECT LEARNING COACH!

Today's life and career coaches don't need to know every sordid detail of your past to help you achieve your goals and dreams today. Likewise, a learning coach needn't know the depths of educational theory or the latest classroom management techniques to become a loving, guiding partner throughout your child's quest toward goals and dreams.

Back in the 1700s, the Earl of Chesterfield wrote to his son: "The young leading the young is like the blind leading the blind; they will both fall into the ditch. The only sure guide is he who has often gone the road which you want to go. Let me be that guide, who has gone all roads, and who can consequently point out to you the best."

There are many compelling reasons that the Earl's advice to his son makes sense, and it helps explain why no one is better suited as learning coach than a caring parent.

- **It's Only Natural.** Since the advent of compulsory schooling about 150 years ago, it has become customary to spend a minimum of thirteen years focusing on children's intellects as they grow. Thanks to this educational approach, during the same period our society slowly but steadily created a proliferation of studied "experts" in every realm possible, including the professionalization of teaching. Placing full confidence in school personnel's expertise, some parents' natural instincts related to child-rearing have atrophied with disuse. When an instinctual "feeling" does strike, we're so used to the focus on intellect that we've grown very good at thinking feelings away.

But consider for a moment who shows baby tigers how to hunt, or little ducklings how to get around the pond. It's a parent, of course! There is nothing more natural and valuable than parental guidance when it comes to helping a human child learn, too.

If you feel your parental instinctive skills could stand a little exercise, not to worry. While using many of the learning coach techniques in this book you'll hone your instincts at the same time.

- **No One Knows Your Child Better.** While retaining the same teacher for several years in elementary grades is an on-going education fad in some sections of the country, more often a teacher charged with educating your child gets to know him— and usually a minimum of twenty or so other children—for ten months. The teacher may take time to review your child's file filled with previous test scores and former teachers' comments in a file, or even learn a thing or two through the more informal grapevine of the teachers' lounge. But that's it.

No one knows your child better than you, the one who watched his personality take shape right before your eyes. You're the one who knows what interests, inspires, and intrigues. You're also the one who knows what aggravates, agitates, and alienates. This information alone lets you help your child better than any Master's degree or textbook or standardized test ever would.

- **Only You Can Eliminate the Perception of a Child "Behind."** Amazing, isn't it, that the perception of a child "falling behind" is so pervasive in our culture that a president uses it to bring attention to his plans to fix educational woes? It was a good choice, though, because it's scary. The perception carries with it a painful, negative, guilt-ridden stigma.

In his bestseller, *The Seven Habits of Highly Effective People*, Stephen R. Covey relates how one of his sons fell victim to Stephen's and his wife Sandra's perceptions of him as "behind": He was socially immature, athletically uncoordinated, and a poor student. Through honest examination of their own feelings, the couple had to admit that even though they loved and cared for the boy, they were trying to help him based on their *own* perception of him as inadequate. The Coveys "began to realize that if we wanted to change the situation, we first had to change ourselves. And to change ourselves effectively, we first had to change our perceptions."

Fellow parents, this is where they unlocked the door to truly helping their child. "We began to *see* our son in terms of his own uniqueness. We *saw* within him layers and layers of potential that would be realized at his own pace and speed. We decided to relax and get out of his way and let his own personality emerge. We *saw* our natural role as being to affirm, enjoy, and value him. We also conscientiously worked on our motives . . . so that our own feelings of worth were not dependent on our children's 'acceptable' behavior."

Like those who employ the learning coach approach within their families, when the Coveys stopped judging and comparing their son, when they stopped measuring him against social expectations, they began to *enjoy* him. And like other children whose parents have shed the perception of "behind," the child flourished.

"As the weeks and months passed . . . he began to blossom, at his own pace and speed," Stephen writes. "He became outstanding as measured by standard social criteria—academically, socially, and athletically—at a rapid clip, far beyond the so-called natural developmental process."

Many of us arrive in the brave new world of parenting completely conditioned to help our children toward success by accepting the school-imposed method of judging and measuring. The act's inevitable outcome is winners and losers, those ahead and those "behind." In your role as parent learning coach, you and your child can leave this detrimental perception behind and move into the wonderful world of acceptance and enjoyment—then watch your baby fly!

- **No One Loves Your Child More.** Yes, many teachers grow to like, value, and respect the children in their classrooms, and they are to be commended. But even the most devoted won't—can't—love and cherish your child as you would.

Julia and Chris' son, Ian, is the third of their four children. At age three he was diagnosed as autistic. Julia characterizes his behavior as "abominable" when it came time to enter kindergarten, and he still didn't speak much. Despite this, "the school services and special education personnel were wonderful," says Chris, "but their focus on the whole word method of learning to read wasn't working for Ian. Knowing and loving Ian as we did, we believed the acquisition of reading skills would make a big difference in his ability and desire to speak."

Julia was surprised at how much Ian enjoyed picking up letter sounds when exposed to a fun phonics program at home at night, "but now I realize it's because he likes symbols." The family "played" patiently together as often as possible for about six months.

"Did you see the movie, *The Miracle Worker*?" Julia asks. "Just as Helen Keller did with water and the sign for it, Ian put together the letter sounds and the word, cat, one night. He took off from there. Now that he's learned to communicate his feelings life is better for all of us. I don't know how long it would have taken if we'd just sat back and waited for the other reading method to work—or if it would have worked at all. We're just so happy now to be able to give—and receive—expressions of love!"

- **No One Cares More about Your Child's Future.** When we're talking about your child's learning experience, we're also talking about her future. There's no one besides her with a greater stake in it than you. After all, when you smooth the way for your child's responsible independence, this means she comes out of the starting gate into adulthood prepared and running, her best shot at a happy, meaningful, productive life. What better insurance that she's not still living at home when she's thirty-five!

DEVELOP A WINNING
LEARNING COACH PERSONALITY

While you don't need a college degree in education to become a learning coach, there are several traits you'll find helpful to your endeavor. Don't worry if you don't possess them in great abundance at the moment. As with your muscles, daily exercise will help build and strengthen them. All you need do is make sure you allow a little time each day to do so. Let's review them so you may start your workout today.

Flexibility

Adults traditionally exert quite a bit of control over children. Yet to be humble enough to guide instead of lead your child, learning coaches should be flexible enough to give up some of that control when it serves the learning purpose. This is not to say, as some mistakenly interpret, that learning coaches allow children to run roughshod over them; they don't. Rather, it means that rigidity can get in the way of a valuable learning opportunity if you let it. This happened to learning-coach-in-training Alexis at least half a dozen times before she caught on.

"I'd spent years establishing routines for eating, sleeping, and studying, so letting go of them was quite uncomfortable at first," says Alexis about life with her two sons now ages ten and twelve. "At first, when we'd make a last minute change in routine to accommodate an activity that was at an unusual time or place for us, it felt like utter chaos and it took two days for me to feel like we were back in rhythm again. But," she adds, "by repeatedly letting go of that control it grew increasingly easier to be more flexible and roll with the circumstances. As a result we're spending more time than ever together as a family because the boys really enjoy what we do because it's based on things they're interested in. Fun and learning at the same time—who would've thought?"

Open mind

Think of learning as performing yoga for your mind, a gentle stretching until your mind can more readily bend in order to wrap around new ways of accomplishing educational goals. This is the trait that lets parents and children alike move beyond the idea that learning only takes place in a school building, and so opens wide the door to every day life as the starting place for learning that really sticks.

Kerry, a Florida mom of three whose youngest is ten years-old, lives where for months each year she had good reason to keep a keen eye on hurricanes. "It wasn't until I started looking beyond textbooks and worksheets to help my kids learn that the thought even occurred to see if my youngest might be interested in helping out," explains Kerry. "So first, I explained to him how to read the barometer. When I went to websites he began looking over my shoulder so we talked some more, about how weather on the continent affects a hurricane's path. Soon I was showing him how to plot coordinates and track the storms. By thinking of opportunities outside of the box of school learning, he enthusiastically picked up a lot of science, plus during the storm season the entire family gets tropical updates four times each day!"

An open mind also helps you remain open to change. You won't need to coach your child long before you become adept at recognizing what works and what doesn't. If everything's working, fine. But if it's not, only an open mind is able to recognize needed change, respond quickly, and alter the situation as needed.

Creativity

Increasing flexibility and opening your mind are exercises guaranteed to help build your creativity, another trait useful to a learning coach. When we want to drop a habit, such as biting nails, talking with our hands, or smoking, we're advised to replace that habit with a healthier one. Similarly, it's easier to drop the habit of thinking that you need to teach in order for your child to learn when you replace it with something else.

Instead of teaching, learning coaches cultivate the ability to recognize something more important—identifying learning moments as they happen. In addition, they cultivate the ability to create new learning moments. It's a task that grows ever easier with practice as Rachel, a long-time learning coach to a son and daughter, now teens, recalls. "I admit it took a while to get out of the habit of sitting them down and saying, "Now, this is what you need and will learn," she says. "Eventually I saw I could be creative and replace that with a minor perspective change. In a nutshell, instead of sitting them down in the family room to learn, I took them out in the community. That's when the creative juices really started to flow. It was so much more fun, too, that the kids quickly learned how to satisfy their own learning needs and my role faded into the background. While at first I was the primary creator, as the kids grew they took on more of the responsibility until my job kind of morphed into consultant/chauffeur."

SAMPLE EXISTING LEARNING MOMENTS

- Use the letters and words on signs all around you for pre-reading and reading practice
- Count, multiply, figure out percentage discounts in department store
- Talk about an election and take your child to the voting booth
- Stay up late (or get up early) and watch the lunar eclipse, shooting stars, or the harvest moon
- Attend city council meeting, nature center demonstration, lecture at library

SAMPLE CREATED LEARNING MOMENTS

- Learn some American Sign Language (ASL) then practice it while waiting in line at the grocery store
- When the child is interested in the new house being built down the street or around the corner, contact the architect and visit office/site
- When it's discussed on the news, get out a map or atlas and find the location of that country your child never heard of
- When a bug flies by, grab paper and crayons and draw a picture of it; learn more about it on the Internet
- When visiting with Grandpa and his friend, ask questions when they talk about the war or their travels to Tibet

Sense of humor

When his teacher noted that seven-year-old Kyle "just wasn't getting" subtraction, Lillian turned to coaching to help her son. After Lillian and Kyle spent the week subtracting everything from digested M&M's to shirts out of the drawer to silverware as it disappeared from the tray, she decided to give him a short handmade test containing about a dozen subtraction problems.

Kyle dutifully sat down at the dining room table and completed it within minutes. "I was thrilled to see he'd answered every single one correctly," says Lillian, "until I realized he'd changed all the subtraction signs to addition signs and they were right *that* way! When I asked Kyle about it he said, 'Aw, Mom, you know I don't like subtraction, so I added the numbers, instead.'"

Some parents might have gotten upset with Kyle's math antics, but Lillian knew that would only add to his math anxiety. Instead, "I laughed and complimented his resourcefulness," Lillian continues. "Then knowing Kyle never saw a challenge he didn't embrace, I stated it had taken two minutes to change all of the signs and do the addition, and wondered out loud how long it would take to change the signs back and do the subtraction. It was just enough of an impetus, offered with a smile, so that he sat back down and worked his way through all the problems. And you know," Lillian says with a giggle, "soon he wasn't having any major problems with it anymore."

Being compelled to do something we don't want to do can at times lead to stress that makes the given task even more difficult to accomplish. Think of the stress when you *had* to have a Pap smear, or serve on a jury, or sit through an IRS audit.

Likewise, the compulsion to attend school, where the act of teaching is taken very seriously, causes stress for many children. In addition, the focus on the intellect ignores the fact that learning is also influenced by emotions, feelings, and attitudes. Children begin to associate their discomfort and imbalance with the act of learning until it becomes an unpleasant—and sometimes downright painful—experience.

The last thing a child in this situation needs is to come home to a Mom or Dad dishing out more of the same serious, stressful approach. At the least, your sense of humor may bring balance to the situation. At the very best, it can help open up your child to the knowledge that learning can take place anywhere, and restore the inate joy of exploration and discovery with which he was born.

Patience

I've saved the trait of patience for last, not because it's least important, but to emphasize that it's not nearly as important as so many learning coaches initially think it would be. Of course you'll need a decent dose of it (what parent doesn't?), but then don't you also need a good shot of patience to deal with co-workers, school teachers and administrators, and sometimes even your spouse?

A Type A personality if ever there was one, I was a confirmed "it's easier and faster to do it myself" person. The thought of turning over everyday household responsibilities to five- to ten-year olds each morning, or making the dreaded grocery shopping trip even longer with such youthful help, or cleaning up after one of them had fed to the cat was, at first, more than I could take. But children do grow into responsibility as surely as they grow into an elder siblings' hand-medowns, and I look back at the time spent as one of the best time investments I could have made in their lives. Not only did they grow comfortable with responsibility, they easily and naturally learned what they needed to know for independent living as young adults. Be it vacuuming or cooking, balancing a checkbook or reinforcing a loose button, mowing a lawn or remembering those less fortunate, devoting those few extra moments each day when they were little served them well. Not only did I wind up with lots of helping hands in the household, I greatly increased my patience quotient in the company of loved ones, and that has served me well, too.

HABITS OF SUCCESSFUL LEARNING COACHES

Just as a handful of personality traits helps make life easier for a learning coach, so too do a few basic habits of behavior also make a difference for the most successful coaches. Horace Mann, considered by some to be the grandaddy of the institutional approach to education, knew very well the power of habit. It is, he said, a cable. "We weave a thread of it every day, and at last we cannot break it." Build the following practices and allow them to serve as the foundation of your efforts, and you're easily and effectively on your way to interesting and exciting days ahead with your child.

Attention and Awareness

Nothing will pay greater dividends than investing as much time as you possibly can in simply observing your child. It's easy to do, too, even as you go about your normal daily routine. You'll learn more about what to watch for in terms of learning styles and multiple intelligences in an upcoming chapter, so right now we'll simply talk about cultivating the habit of being attentive and aware.

So many aspects of our lives, whether it's the way we begin our mornings or prepare meals or go about our children's bedtimes, become so completely routine, we can easily accomplish them by rote. Each time we engage in activity on autopilot, however, we're not attentive ("paying attention, observant, listening"). Yet we must be attentive to be aware ("conscious, cognizant, fully informed") so we can pick up the helpful clues about how our children learn best that often are right under our noses, if only we're prepared to see them.

"I saved so much time learning about Zachariah (age ten) just by paying attention to how he fills his spare time," says Laurie, a single mom of two who works two jobs to make ends meet. "While at some level I knew he was always taking things apart, intent on fixing them, I never noticed how frequently he did so and with such diligence and patience. I realized he has to touch and explore and see how the pieces fit together in order to understand how things work. And," Laurie adds, "that includes how a clock ticks."

Laurie began to understand that her son needed to be actively engaged and in motion in order to learn. She stopped trying to make Zachariah sit down when she helped him with his homework. "I planned our precious one week vacation in the Gettysburg area so we could walk and he could touch and explore the environment as we learned about the history he needed to know. I kept on-hand a wide array of manipulatives for math so he could actually do the problems with his hands. What a difference."

Develop the habits of attention and awareness to make coaching much easier for you.

OBSERVE!

Here is a starting list of things to watch for.
You'll think of many more as you acquire the habit
of observation.

- How does your child fill free time?
- What makes him happiest?
- What gets him stressed out?
- When tackling something new, does she learn more
  easily when she sees, hears, touches, or has a combination
  of all three?
- Does your child prefer to be alone when working on
  something, or prefer to have you or friends or siblings
  present?
- Does your child follow directions better when you tell
  him, or show him what needs to be done?
- Quiet, or the hub-bub of family life while studying?
- When she knows she needs to remember something,
  does she sit down and concentrate or never really settle
  down at all?

These are your first clues to determine:
- What types of learning materials will likely be most
  effective
- An optimum learning environment
- The best way to guide, inspire, and mentor your child

Discover and use interests to customize education

Your observations will reveal some of the most useful information a learning coach can receive. You'll discover your child's interests— you know, those topics that always capture her attention when she hears about them, those things she just can't stop talking about. Whether it's trains, castles, dogs, cats, spiders, fire engines, space ships, rocks, comics, baseball, soccer, or guitars, these are perfect starting points for customizing education.

Elaine's eight year-old daughter Lennon hated reading, but she loved Care Bears. So Elaine scoured her local discount store and drug store for every Care Bear book she could find —reading books, yes, but also sticker, activity, and coloring books. Then she simply left them around the house; on the coffee table, kitchen counter, bathroom shelf, and even in the car.

"At first," Elaine explains, "Lennon just played with the stickers and coloring books. But sure enough she started picking up the picture books and leafing through them, until one day she began asking me what individual words were. She was teaching herself how to read!"

Soon Lennon would read aloud to her Mom, either voluntarily or with little prompting. "I was worried that I'd run out of Care Bear materials for her," Elaine continues, "but I needn't have been. With the desire to learn and growing ability to read, Lennon saw there were many other things she wanted to know about, and we moved on to the exotic animals she loves. Now we're reading short non-fic- tion books about them and pasting pictures of them on their country of origin on a giant world map. She's doing a great job of sounding out the names of African countries when she learns them."

Don't forget to exercise your creativity to expand your child's inter- ests. You can pique your child's curiosity in many topics simply by introducing them in a fun, different, interesting manner. A science textbook tells about insects; an ant farm and magnifying glass invites your child into their world. Gandhi is a name in a history book; watch the movie together and he turns into a human being. A worksheet about compasses is a bunch of arrows; rent a boat, lose sight of shore, and a compass becomes the thread connecting your child to safety.

COACH'S MOTIVATIONAL MINUTE: Always remember that your child may (probably!) learn in a very different way than you do. Every individual is unique and brings to the learning experience his own viewpoint and experience. Keep in mind, too, that what works well with one child won't necessarily work well with another.

Encourage independence through the child's active role in education

It's often difficult to visualize a child taking strides toward independence when he's still just a youngster. That's why it helps aspiring learning coaches when experienced moms like Erin, whose oldest of three children is seventeen, shares what she's witnessed after a decade of coach-like behavior.

Erin watched helplessly when her older daughter, Jody, entered her third year of high school and a world that included too little homework and too much petty trouble that was rapidly escalating in quality and quantity. While discussing the problem one evening, Erin understood her daughter's frustration with mixed messages. "They [school personnel] treat us like babies," said Jody, "always telling us where to go and what to do and what to think. At least with my friends they're *my* decisions, what I choose to do and when."

Instead of entering into a shouting match, or threatening to ground Jody, or otherwise setting up a no-win situation for both mother and daughter, Erin chose to directly address the root of the problem and suggested that she and Jody work together to create opportunities to exercise the naturally and normally growing desire for independence welling up inside the teen.

"First, Jody took some time to consider what she might want to do if granted more independent time. She loves to write, so spending some of the time that way was a no-brainer," says Erin. "But she was also interested in starting her own business, so she made a list of local entrepreneurs who interested her. When she visited the third one, an ad agency whose owner was quite receptive to the idea of an apprentice, she was so psyched she couldn't sleep at night."

"Next," Erin continues, "we had to increase the time she could spend away from the situation she felt was stifling her. We worked with the guidance counselor to rearrange her classes to group all of the 'lost time' together at the end of the day, including lunch, and through a work-study program, got her out of school just before 1PM, at which time each day she went to the ad agency where, I might add, she got additional chances to exercise her desire to write."

Within a few months Erin realized she was dealing with a brand new Jody. "Her sense of responsibility grew and her grades improved," says Erin. "More importantly her hunger for independence was satiated and she made new, adult friends. She grew less interested in the lure of late nights and the trouble associated with them. Before my eyes an uninspired, troubled little girl turned into a happy, confident young woman."

You don't need to wait until your child becomes a teen to build independence. In fact, that may be too late. Encourage and support interests while your child is still young, and through his attention and active role in learning, his independence will grow as quickly as his feet.

Lose the illusion of an educational "finish line"

Another problem that is seldom, if ever, addressed contributed to Jody's teen year turmoil. The problem is the pervasive idea that kids are racing toward some imaginary "finish line" of education. We can't blame the kids; the way the system works both creates and encourages the dilemma.

While still very young, a child becomes aware of the concept that he will go to a specific place to learn. He eventually realizes that, like the "big kids" he sees waiting at neighborhood bus stops, he will go to the specific place until he, too, is almost out of his teen years. Then, through the issuance of a diploma, he no longer needs to go to the specific place anymore. This changes many a child's perspective on learning, just as it did for Jody.

"Jody was convinced that she was almost 'done' learning," Erin remembers, "and it contributed greatly to her growing apathy. I shamefully admit my exhortations to just keep your head together and hang in there, you're almost done, helped fuel that concept. When she got to know people out and about in the business world it completely turned around her thinking. She could see they're always reading trade magazines, taking classes, learning new computer programs, and discussing new trends and ideas to figure out how to implement them in their own business."

Jody's educational choices, made independently of schooling, put her in a position to see, up-close and personal, how learning continues to fill the lives of successful adults. School work grew more palatable as she realized it was an endurable, if not enjoyable, piece of a much longer journey, not a final destination that didn't make any sense to her.

When you as coach lose the illusion of an educational finish line you help your child keep schooling in perspective. Instead of viewing learning as a temporary aberration, you place it into context as a life-long process that unfolds in the greater world, as a natural aspect of a fulfilling life.

COACH'S INSPIRATIONAL MINUTE: When you feel the urge to slip into teaching mode, put your time to better use by replacing that habit with any of the following or other ideas you'll discover soon.

JOURNAL: Observe your child for clues about the way he learns, and then date and write them down; they'll be helpful in the future.

GUIDE: Think of yourself like a tour guide, not one who defines the journey but rather points the way and otherwise works to ensure that the trip is rewarding.

NETWORK: You can't take advantage of all the community has to offer if you don't stay connected and in touch with what's going on.

CREATE: What would be a fun and/or unusual way for your child to learn about fractions, a foreign country, parts of a plant, or the Civil War? Create that opportunity.

INSPIRE, ENCOURAGE, AND SUPPORT LEARNING: The easiest way to do this is to begin with what your child shows interest in.

INTEGRATE LEARNING INTO DAILY LIFE: Think outside of the box, the school box, that is. Learning happens everywhere.

WORK YOUR WAY OUT OF A JOB: With every skill your child acquires you're one more step along the way to retirement from being a learning coach!

CHAPTER 3

LET'S GET THE COACH IN SHAPE!

Like many other parents, Judy, a mother of two girls in first and third grades, pulls me aside after my workshop presentation. "Everything you say about helping your kids learn 'feels' so right, but . . ."

Judy finishes her sentence with, "I don't think I'm smart enough." Other common endings include, I don't think I'm patient enough, I don't think I have enough money, I don't think I have enough time, I wouldn't know where to start, or I'm afraid my child is already too far gone.

"How old are your girls?" I ask.

"Seven and ten," Judy answers.

"And they don't know how to use the toilet?" I ask.

"Of course they do!" says Judy, a bit indignantly.

Do they walk? (Yes.) Talk? (Yes.) Feed themselves? (Yes.) Throw a ball? (Yes.) Tie their sneakers? (Yes.) Ride bikes? (Yes.) The look on

Judy's face tells me to stop my fairly lengthy list of questions here.

"How did they learn so many skills, especially such complicated ones as walking and talking?" I ask.

"I helped them, of course. I'm their mother!" Judy is almost shouting.

"Were your walking classes held at the same time every day? Did you give them a written test on self-feeding? How many hours of bike-riding homework did you assign each day?" Judy looks perplexed.

"Judy, you didn't *teach* your girls in the way your own schooling has trained you to think of teaching," I explain. "What you *did* do was seize on their desire to learn—when the time was right—to guide their learning. You may *think* you're not smart enough, and I would suggest you examine where such a ludicrous idea came from, but what I'm saying is to forget the idea of "teaching" and instead *continue* to help your daughters learn, very much the same way you've already done for years." The smile spreading across Judy's face tells me she understands.

Does the idea of becoming your child's learning coach give you the jitters, too? Are you worried because you think you'll need to memorize the Periodic Table of Elements or know how to solve a quadratic equation in your head? You may conjure up visions of mutating into an Albert Einstein clone, but the truth is that he wouldn't have made nearly as good a learning coach for your child as you can be. Despite Mr. Einstein's genius, he couldn't have cared as deeply or become as invested in your child's life, of which her education is a part, as you are. (Remember, a major contributing factor to genius is abundant love.)

You'll begin getting in shape as a coach by letting go of preconceived notions, usually based on your own educational experience, of what a teacher must do, clearing the way for the distinctively different coach concept to guide your efforts. Next, many coaches agree there are a few basic steps that, once integrated into your family life, help promote academic success, as well as keep the experience fun. C'mon, let's go get in shape!

THE VITAL DIFFERENCES BETWEEN TEACHING AND COACHING

The learning coach capitalizes on a child's curiosity and interests to create enthusiasm for learning and clues to customize his education

Grasp this concept and you're well on your way to understanding the nuances of the differences between teaching and coaching because it supplies the foundation upon which you will build awareness. Remember the sentence: Curiosity creates interest, interest increases attention to the task at hand, and attention gives rise to learning.

If you talk to ten parents who use the learning coach approach, you'll likely find at least one like Amber, who chose this alternative because of a perceived attention deficit in her then first grader son, Jackson. "Given the opportunity, young children can follow their trains of thought and imaginations for an incredibly long way," says Amber. "Contrary to popular belief, little ones have quite long attention spans. When they're interested in a project just try to distract them—and shame on you if you do!"

Amber recalls that it was quite simple. If she just observed and listened to Jackson, now eight-years old, for even brief periods of time she easily uncovered what he was curious about at any given time. Take a recent learning odyssey, for example—sea creatures. After watching a television program on the subject, Jackson had many questions, and the learning team went to work to find the answers through the Internet, library books and magazines for both children and adults, and a couple of videos they found at their local video rental store. Any parent would have been proud of the interest-driven attention and subsequent learning about science that was taking place, but Amber decided to push the envelope.

The mother-son learning team was collecting so much information—articles, photos, maps, Jackson's drawings, and more —Amber went to the local office supply store and purchased a large three-ring binder and filled it with a colorful, heavy stock paper onto which the team carefully glued and taped their materials. She says, "Interest propelled Jackson to dictate stories to me to accompany his favorite pictures. I printed out his stories on the computer in a large, easy to read font, and Jackson spent hours practicing his handwriting by copying them to put in his rapidly growing notebook. When he created a map of a fictional sea where his favorite creatures lived together, he learned about directions and scale in the process."

Amber applied just three slight changes from the traditional approach of instruction:

- **Being aware and attentive.** She recognized Jackson's curiosity that manifested itself as interest in a particular topic.

- **Using interest to customize the learning experience.** As you'll see from a multitude of examples presented in this book, the specific topic of interest doesn't matter; what matters is that the subsequent learning experience is meaningful to the child.

- **Aiding her son's interest-driven learning instead of instructing him.** Jackson's attentiveness created a large field on which additional learning grew (Jackson not only learned about sea creatures, but also voluntarily, eagerly, and happily engaged in creative writing, handwriting practice, and map skills).

The learning coach encourages independence through an active role in education

Although there are many ways in which to teach a child something, traditional classroom teaching is something done *to* a learner. Guided by the school's curriculum that predetermines which pieces of knowledge should be imparted at a particular grade level, a teacher then gives this information to the students. The student's role is to receive said information, then demonstrate retention through quizzes, tests, essays, etc.

The learning coach doesn't do or give something *to* the child. Rather, she preserves the student's active role in his education by facilitating *his* learning. She does this by clearing difficulties or obstacles out of his way, and aiding and assisting his own efforts in every way possible. In other words, she helps make the trip toward "academic all-star" as easy as possible.

Betsy, a part-time chef, knew her eleven-year-old daughter, Denise, was bored in her fifth grade class, not only because of her declining grades, but because Denise shared the news with anyone who would listen. "She didn't like the subjects or having to sit and listen while the teacher explained the same things over and over again," says Betsy. "So one day, after she complained to her uncle about how much she hates the books she has to read for class, I asked what she'd rather read. She had no idea."

Betsy told Denise that while she had to continue reading assigned material there was no reason she couldn't do that quickly, then turn to literature of her own choosing. Betsy checked the Internet for titles recommended for pre-teens and brought the list and Denise to the library once a week before work. "At first," explains Betsy, "she checked out at least ten books each week, only to start them, determine they weren't any good, and move on to the next batch. But after she read *The Midwife's Apprentice* by Karen Cushner, which she knew was on our recommended list, she started looking up recommendations on the Internet herself!"

That wasn't all. The story, set in the Middle Ages, sparked Denise's interest in the time period. Her Internet searches for related recommendations cut down considerably the number of frustrating false starts Denise previously experienced when looking for a good read.

In addition, she discovered the Society for Creative Anachronism, an organization dedicated to researching and re-creating pre-seventeenth century European history and, as a resident of "The Kingdom of the East," delighted in finding out more about heraldry, combat and chivalry, and taking part in the society's social gatherings where her imagination and creativity flourished.

The learning coach encourages a broader vision of learning

If the teacher's job is "to give instruction to," it logically follows that there must be a stopping point. This leads us to believe, if only subconsciously, that learning is dependent on a teacher, therefore, the end of "teaching" marks an end to learning. The long term effects of this reaction to the unspoken message of dependence on someone else to learn results in adults who stop pursuing knowledge upon graduation, feeling as if they reached "the finish line."

The short-term effect of this illusion afflicts the lives of many children, like Naomi's nine-year-old son, Peter. "At the end of the day," Naomi remembers, "Peter was so burned out he thumbed his nose at anything that even hinted at being educational, including television programs, stating that there were so many things he *had* to learn that he didn't want to learn anything else! I knew I had to help him change his views on education fast."

Naomi realized any blatant attempts would be summarily rejected, "so I was gentle while pointing him toward a larger perspective. The good thing is he likes to talk," explains Naomi, "so putting a little effort into guiding conversation was much easier than 'teaching' him. When he talked about baseball, I told him I never understood all those statistics in the newspaper. He was happy to show me what he understood, and together we figured out what he didn't. We wound up covering math skills usually reserved for higher grade levels. When he talked about the Harry Potter book he was reading, I mentioned it must be fun for the author to make up so many new words. Being silly, we started to make up our own, then figure out how the word might be used—as a name of something or someone, as something one would do, or as a description. Soon we were making up sentences for each other's words, watching to make sure it was used as a noun, verb, or adjective as the creator suggested."

Naomi is well on her way to becoming adept at weaving "lessons" into her family's existing way of life.

The learning coach assesses progress without tests, essays, and research papers

As a learning coach focused on *aiding* your child's learning, the need to assess progress based on other children is eliminated. When you think about it, that sort of comparison would no longer even make sense, as the goal of assessment is no longer to measure receipt of instruction. You might view it as taking the spotlight off the instruction, and shining it on the learner, instead. Progress is now measured in terms of personal growth, by whether or not your individual child is moving forward on his own growth path. What other children may or may not know how to do, or how many of them know more or less than your child, is irrelevant to your coaching.

"I have to admit this was the biggest stumbling block to successful coaching for me," says Julia, the mother of six-year-old twin girls. "We're so conditioned to look at education as a competition between ourselves and our classmates it was hard to stop thinking in terms of where the girls were compared to, say, the kids next door, or the 'smartest' kid in the class. It didn't hit home until I heard you say in your workshop, 'Education isn't some race your child is running —it's your beautiful, special, unique child's *life!*' I sometimes slip back into that comparison mode," Julia confesses, "but I'm working at it and more often I'm able to recognize—and appreciate—the remarkable number of things the girls are learning, mostly because I'm watching *them* and not some pretty limited yard-stick somebody else set out for children. Where once I saw two mediocre students now I see two girls moving forward."

I hope you're feeling more relaxed and confident about being your child's learning coach. Your confidence will grow even greater as you realize your knowledge of the unique individual who is your child will guide your actions. An important step, therefore, is to gather this knowledge as quickly and thoroughly as possible. Learning coaches agree this makes your job easier and your efforts that much more effective.

GROW TRUST IN AND RESPECT FOR YOUR CHILD THROUGH TIME AND ATTENTION

Have you heard of the football coach who spends only one hour each week with his players? Or the business coach who manages from his couch? These are silly notions. Like other coaches, learning coaches also need to devote as much time and attention to their "players" as possible. That said, coaching isn't a full-time job for which you need to set aside other aspects of life, either. Rather, it's a matter of s-t-r-e-t-c-h-i-n-g the time you spend with your child, and being attentive to your goals during whatever amount of time is available to you. This is the best way to get to truly know your child. What makes him smile? Laugh? Get angry? What are his hopes and dreams? His worst nightmare? What inspires him? What is he curious about? What does he like to create? Why? Is he a social butterfly, or does he entrench himself in a rich, inner world? Who are his best friends? Why does he like them? Who is his hero? Why? If he could choose to go anywhere in the world, what destination would he pick? You get the idea.

Just as with your friends or your boss or your new beau, the more you know about your child, the better you understand him. The better you understand him, the easier it becomes to trust and respect him, and this will be returned, in kind.

Remembering and reflecting

Ah, the wisdom of the saying, "Before you judge, walk a mile in his moccasins." You can squeeze yourself into your child's sneakers simply by remembering and reflecting on what it's like to be a child. Learning coaches say this is a powerful exercise that opens their eyes and hearts at the same time.

"When I was really caught up in problems at work and the daily repetitive needs of my family," admits Lauren, "I thought of Tonya's complaints about school, people, homework, or anything else for that matter as simply petty."

But over the next couple of weeks, Lauren made the effort to dig into her memory bank for remembrances of her own eleventh year—where she was, who her friends were, what was important to her. "I realized those 'petty' things Tonya was trying to talk about are the center of her universe," she says. "And if *I* didn't pay attention, who would? After that, it became a lot easier to put down my own baggage for a little while, listen better and, as a result, we grew a lot closer."

Mary and her husband, Paul, often found themselves at wit's end with the antics of three healthy boys, ages six, ten, and twelve. "One of us was always telling one of them to do this, or not do that," Paul says, "and it seemed like a holler fest from the time we got up until we got out the door, then again in the evening until they went to bed. There was never any peace."

"Spencer, our youngest, wasn't feeling well and was lying with his head on his dad's lap and asked, 'What was the world like when you were little, Dad?'" Mary recalls. "Paul told Spencer he didn't remember much, and this bothered Paul. He must have really been reflecting on it because at the oddest times he would have these 'Eureka' moments and blurt out things like, 'I used to catch frogs in the pond down the road and bring them home to scare my sisters,' and 'I took the vitamin pills my mother gave me and stuffed them into the cracks along the steps that went upstairs!'"

These events helped both Paul and Mary see their sons' behavior from a different perspective. "They weren't purposely trying to give us gray hair," Paul laughs, "they were being young boys. All of a sudden, we didn't just holler anymore. Our correction was backed by understanding, understanding that we relayed to the boys. It made a world of difference in our home environment."

You, too, can spend odd moments of your day or night remembering what it was like to be a child—the challenges, the interests, the tribulations, the triumphs. This will help you trust that your child, who may seem like hell on two wheels, isn't necessarily on the path to self-destruction but rather testing the same waters you did at a similar age. When you trust and respect your child's current intellectual and emotional standing, you become a much more effective learning coach.

Learning to understand and accept your child as is

In a world where competition to enter college begins with the right preschool, it's easy for parents to slip into the habit of comparing their children's abilities and accomplishments to those of other children. This tendency leads us to think more about what our children *can* be instead of what they *are* at this wonderful moment in time.

Nine-year-old Jacob's dad paid for his own college attendance with a football scholarship, then played the game professionally for a few years. He couldn't understand his son's lack of interest—and coordination—and drove himself and the boy crazy when he whipped out a football every time they spent a few moments together. Stephanie, mom to Jacob and four other children, knew they were on a collision course.

"I started gently," she says, "occasionally pointing out to my husband the things at which Jacob excels, including his warm, nurturing side and his help with his siblings. I encouraged him to do things together that Jacob enjoys, like creating with Legos and building model cars, and to include Jacob in his projects around the house. It took a little while, but I began noticing that at night before we went to sleep my husband said things like, 'Jacob was a big help with the yard work this afternoon' and 'Did you see how fast he's coming along with that new model car?' His perception of Jacob as inept was being replaced with one of competence. As my husband's respect for Jacob grew they began spending more time together until at some imperceptible point football was no longer an issue."

Sure, Jacob isn't going to quarterback his way into college, but Dad found he is a smart, capable, likeable young man in his own right, in his own way. Jacob is flourishing with the support and encouragement resulting from Dad's perspective change.

COACH'S MOTIVATIONAL MINUTE: Remember the last time someone recognized and commented on something you did well. The good feeling that comment brought about lasted far longer than the comment itself. Children spend a lot of time in situations where the focus is on what they do wrong. Not only will they grow smarter when someone pays attention to what they do right, you may find they'll be a lot healthier and happier, too.

Throughout this book you'll find many more stories, ideas, and techniques that will help you help your child grow and thrive. But first, spend a bit of time concentrating on, recognizing, and celebrating who she is at this very moment in time.

CHAPTER 4

PUTTING POPULAR LEARNING THEORIES TO WORK

You're observing and recognizing many of the habits and qualities that, gathered together, make your child the unique person she is. Lucky for us the growing interest in brain development and learning also gives parents the information we need to determine which intelligences and learning styles combine in those unique persons in our care. Consider this a crash course, some basics to get you started, with a recommendation that you read any or all of the books listed in this section for increased understanding.

RECOMMENDED READING ON LEARNING STYLES AND MULTIPLE INTELLIGENCES

- *In Their Own Way: Discovering and Encouraging Your Child's Personal Learning Style*, Thomas Armstrong, Ph.D.

- *Awakening Your Child's Natural Genius: Enhancing Curiosity, Creativity, and Learning Ability*, Thomas Armstrong, Ph.D.

- *Flow: The Psychology of Optimal Experience*, Mihaly Csikszentmihalyi

- *Frames of Mind: The Theory of Multiple Intelligences*, Howard Gardner

- *The Unschooled Mind: How Children Think and How Schools Should Teach*, Howard Gardner

- *A Mind at a Time*, Mel Levine

- *Seven Times Smarter: 50 Activities, Games, and Projects to Develop the Seven Intelligences of Your Child*, Laurel Schmidt

- *Discover Your Child's Learning Style*, Mariemma Willis and Victoria Kindle Hodson

THE THEORY OF MULTIPLE INTELLIGENCES

One of the greatest contributions to the modern understanding of learning just may be the theory of multiple intelligences, brought to us by Harvard University psychologist Howard Gardner. In a nutshell, Mr. Gardner urges parents and educators alike to identify and value eight different "intelligent ways of thinking." In *Intelligence Reframed: Multiple Intelligences for the 21st Century* Gardner defines intelligence as "a biopsychological potential to process information that can be activated in a cultural setting to solve problems or create products that are of value in a culture." This definition helps us realize that different intelligences become important depending on the setting and the task at hand. (See the box for a brief overview of the eight intelligences). If you found yourself in a survival situation, for example, you'd be happy to possess, or have with you another who possesses, a high degree of bodily-kinesthetic intelligence in order to leap tall banana trees in a single bound. If your group is unable to move ahead on a project because of major differences in opinions of what to do next, someone high in interpersonal intelligence, a good communicator and natural mediator, could be your ticket to moving forward.

AN OVERVIEW OF THE EIGHT MULTIPLE INTELLIGENCES

- **LINGUISTIC:** This child thinks in words; possesses good auditory skills; learns best by hearing and seeing words or by verbalizing
- **LOGICAL-MATHEMATICAL:** This child thinks conceptually; enjoys patterns and experimenting
- **BODILY-KINESTHETIC:** This child processes knowledge through bodily sensations; possesses fine motor coordination; learns best by moving or acting things out

- **VISUAL-SPATIAL:** This child thinks in pictures and images; likely to be artistic and/or inventive
- **MUSICAL:** This child possesses talent for creating and/ or a high appreciation of music (includes singing); is sensitive to nonverbal sounds and may hear sounds that others don't
- **INTERPERSONAL:** This child is a good organizer, communicator, and/or mediator; learns best by relating and cooperating with others
- **INTRAPERSONAL:** This child is deeply aware of inner ideas and feelings; reveals signs of inner wisdom or intuition and deep sense of self
- **NATURALIST:** This child is a good classifier; skilled at observing, understanding, and organizing patterns in the natural environment; able to analyze miniscule differences, such as fingerprint variations or the sounds of different engines
- **NOTE:** All of the intelligences are present in everyone, but in different combinations, so several of the descriptions should fit your child.

The long-standing learning culture of school is built largely on the lecture and textbook forms of information delivery. Because of this it almost exclusively values just two of the intelligences, linguistic and logical-mathematical. As a result, those who possess the whopping 75 percent of undervalued intelligences often experience a variety of problems in school. In *A Mind at a Time*, Dr. Mel Levine wrote, "Parents can take solace in the well-documented finding that report cards are notoriously poor at predicting how your child will eventually do in a career . . . Parents need to find things to praise in a struggling child and make sure that he doesn't give up on himself and get depressed and distressed while waiting for his day to come."

COACH'S MOTIVATIONAL MINUTE: Keeping your child "future oriented" in the face of school problems just may be more important than raising his grade on a spelling test from a D to a C. As your child's learning coach you can use knowledge of his intelligences to pry open the narrow approach to learning. You provide hope by developing his strengths, understanding that nurtured strengths will serve him well in forums other than school and in adult life, using his strengths to shore up his weaknesses, and generally letting him know that his gifts are valued at home and elsewhere.

Maggie feels her twelve-year-old son, Kyle, benefited from attention to his innate strength just in time. She had seen his grades plummet throughout the years and she began to fear one day he would either drop out or be kicked out of school. "It seemed Kyle could fix anything around the house for as long as I can remember," explains Maggie, "so I knew he was no dummy. But the worse he did in school, the more he hated it. Or the more he hated it, the worse he did. I don't know which came first, but it all just spiraled out of control."

Then one day, after Kyle fixed his senior citizen neighbor's lawn-mower, the man offered to introduce him to some friends who also needed occasional help with similar matters. News of Kyle's special gift spread by word of mouth, and it wasn't long before Kyle was working on one to three projects each week. Grateful recipients refused to take no for an answer and paid him for his efforts.

"Kyle's attitude changed," says his mom, "including his approach to school. I know people worry that work takes kids' time away from study, but in this case it actually helps Kyle. It's the first thing in a long time that lets him feel smart, useful, and talented, to experience success and honest appreciation. We're already checking into vocational and other alternative high school options for him—his innate intelligence should be celebrated, not ignored."

As a result of his work, Howard Gardner has become a proponent of what he calls "individually configured education." As if to underscore the importance of your efforts as a learning coach, in *Intelligence Reframed* Gardner writes that "a moment's thought reveals the essential inequity in the uniform school," where the false assumption that all individuals are the same extends equally falsely to the idea that all students are being reached "equally and equitably." He continues, "Knowing the minds of students represents but the first step. Crucial, thereafter, is an effort to draw on this knowledge in making decisions about curriculum, pedagogy, and assessment." This is just what you're going to be able to do after you get in shape, learning coach!

WAYS OF LEARNING UNVEILED

As the amount of research confirming that we learn best in different ways multiplies so, too, do the number of ways in which to look at the styles. Here is a very condensed look at just two of those ways. Those who favor a workbook approach might enjoy the method developed by educators Willis and Kindle Hodson in *Discover Your Child's Learning Style*. They've created a do-it-yourself profile so parents of children six years of age and older can examine five aspects of improving education: disposition, talents, interests, modality, and environment. They also recommend that you, as parent, take the profile, too, and I heartily agree. When you see how your own preferences differ from your child's, you just may find yourself worrying a lot less and avoiding unnecessary conflict.

TIPS TO YOUR CHILD'S LEARNING DISPOSITION
(ACCORDING TO WILLIS AND KINDLE HODSON)

Note how the dispositions mirror and support the idea of multiple intelligences.

- **IF YOUR CHILD IS** *PERFORMING*—He's often known as the class clown or family tease and will do whatever necessary to get an audience. Can be mistaken as hyperactive or having Attention Deficit Hyperactivity Disorder (ADHD). Typically bright, witty, and outspoken, rules and agreements can fall by the wayside and may often find himself in trouble.
  How to Inspire—Provide space, challenge, unscheduled time, and projects that let him move, act, and do. After fifteen to twenty minutes of sitting down it's time for a break. Reinforce subject material and skills with activities that provide opportunity to run, jump, skip, hop, or dance. Use timelines, charts, jokes, rhymes, and riddles. Assess his

learning through skits, performances, presentations, funny songs, pantomime, and audio or video "productions."

- **IF YOUR CHILD IS** *PRODUCING*—This child is likely appreciated in the classroom because she is organized, neat, efficient, and on time. Very willing to tackle assignments, if only for the pleasure of completion, she enjoys schedules, lists, and planning.
  How to Inspire—Provide quiet, routine, order, and predictability. Effective learning materials are sequential and logical (think workbooks), and a "due date" doesn't hurt. She'll strive toward goals, so help her set them frequently. Use materials that bring order to information; calendars, portfolios, timelines, contracts, research papers, graphs, outlines, recipes, and more. While she likes routine, everyone needs a bit of fun as a break once in a while. Assess her learning through goal achievement, grades, and gold stars.

- **IF YOUR CHILD IS** *INVENTING*—This child loves to experiment, and organization neatness, and efficiency don't count nearly as much as creativity and uniqueness of the solution to a problem. He's the "absent-minded professor" who's late for appointments, not because he's rude but because he's so engrossed and focused on a project he doesn't have any idea of how much time has transpired. This child may well prefer solitary to group work, but likes to brainstorm and debate. Often, the need to find a solution to a problem keeps him reading when otherwise he might not. Inquisitive, smart, and competent, age mates might view him as a teacher's pet or nerd.

How to Inspire—Provide lots of opportunity for discovery, questioning, designing new solutions, and time for exploration. Use materials that present varied ideas, theories, and models. Apply the scientific method whenever possible. Help child learn to analyze, predict, visualize, examine, compare and contrast, draw conclusions, classify, and categorize. Provide visual and/or hands-on information. Assess learning through debate, drawing, model construction, experiment results.

- **IF YOUR CHILD IS** *RELATING/INSPIRING*—This child is perceptive, highly emotional, sensitive to others' feelings, compassionate, and values teamwork. Happiest while helping others, she's also chatty and "in touch" with everything going on around her (even if it means spending countless hours on the telephone or her parents thinking her friends are far too important to her). Her own feelings are easily crushed, and she may be on too many teams or committees. Depends upon others for support.

How to Inspire—Present concepts in terms of social events (she's an American Indian and the Pilgrims have just landed, for example), biographies, and stories and fables. Also provide opportunity to debate, compare, voice opinions, defend or justify, make differentiations. Assess learning via discussion, oral presentations, journals, or role-playing the people involved in history, math and science, etc.

- **IF YOUR CHILD IS** *THINKING/CREATIVE*—This child is

similar to the Inventing child, minus the need to think about or create something concrete. Rather, he is more interested in inspiring or instructing, often in a philosophical manner. This child can also garner the title of ADD or ADHD because he often appears to be dreaming, or may doodle or look out the window during lessons. He is content alone and can entertain himself for a long period of time, so may appear withdrawn or even shy.

How to Inspire—Give this child plenty of time to think and dream and provide materials with philosophical or artistic aspects with an opportunity to exercise the creative process. Know that if he's doodling, it may actually be helping him pay attention. He enjoys learning through poetry, art, literature, or drama, and the chance to design, compose, find a different way to do something, or engage in creative writing. Assess learning via artistic presentations such as poems, collages, paintings or scale models, surveys, journals, or timelines.

"I'm the kind of person who reads the directions first," says Dotty, "so it drove me crazy when we would assemble something new and Sara, my seven-year old, would rip apart the little bags with six hundred pieces and jump into the project, seemingly without thinking first. It got to the point where I didn't want to do anything like that with her. It was actually a relief to find out we have different dispositions and how normal that is. I was beginning to think there was something terribly wrong with my daughter!"

Perhaps you'd be more comfortable viewing the different ways of learning in terms of Dr. Mel Levine's eight neurodevelopmental systems. Everyone knows "learning" occurs in the brain, but how does it work? Here, for your enlightenment, is a brief, magical mystery tour.

Brains are made up of two kinds of cells: nerve cells (neurons), with branches called dendrites, and glial cells. The glial cells nourish the billions of neurons that busily create and maintain connections for thinking. This is accomplished when a neuron's dendrites pick up messages from other neurons and send them to the cell's body, from which the message travels further still to the axon, the neuron's "out box." When leaving the out box, the message must "jump" across a gap (synapse) to be picked up by another neuron's dendrites. This feat occurs billions of times each day as we participate in mental activity.

Enter new experiences for a child. These new experiences create new connections, changing the structure of dendrites and synapses to create new paths down which messages may travel. A child learns new skills as the brain becomes more flexible now that alternative paths to the old destinations are developing. Experience, then, in all of its many manifestations, is key to learning.

In *A Mind at a Time,* Dr. Levine explains, "At any point, the strength of functions within each system directly influences performance in and out of school." As in Howard Gardner's theory, Dr. Levine says everyone possesses a combination of strong and weaker systems. Part of his message to parents is that awareness of all the systems will help you see where your child's development may be speeding right along, lacking, or temporarily halted. This is an unjustly brief look at Dr. Levine's work (you can read *A Mind at a Time* to get the whole scoop), so let me add that he notes strengths and weaknesses can change over time, often through consistent exercise (or lack thereof). Equally important for a learning coach to remember: "Some profiles work better at certain ages than at others. Sometimes the very same traits that jeopardize your kid in third grade could evolve into his prize assets during adulthood. Distractibility and daydreaming during reading class may be an attention deficit yet may also be early indicators of creativity and innovative thinking, 'symptoms' that will bolster her career as a scriptwriter or music video producer."

As the notion of "geniuses" we visited in Chapter 1 reminds us, children allowed the freedom of time and mind to nurture their "symptoms" often put them to wonderful use as adults. As learning coach you need to remember to keep your child's schooling in perspective. Yes, it will be wonderful when your efforts raise report card grades. But education is much broader and deeper than this, and your goal is to improve, enliven, and put joy in your child's education, *not* just increase test scores. Keep improved grades in perspective by looking at them as the tip of iceberg. The broader, more important education picture lies below, and is impossible to reveal through test scores.

DR. LEVINE'S NEURODEVELOPMENTAL SYSTEMS

- ATTENTION CONTROL SYSTEM—attention keeps your child focused while filtering out distractions
- MEMORY SYSTEM—much more memory is needed for school success than is required in virtually any career
- LANGUAGE SYSTEM—includes phonics, vocabulary, expressing written and oral thoughts, comprehension of verbal instructions and explanations, and second languages
- SPATIAL ORDERING SYSTEM—the wiring designed to discern patterns and discriminate between them
- SEQUENTIAL ORDERING SYSTEM—a partner of spatial ordering, addresses chains of information coming into or going out of the brain; on a higher plane, involved in reasoning
- MOTOR SYSTEM—governs the precise and complex network of connections between the brain and various body muscles; includes sports performance, but also the physical act of writing, using scissors, playing an instrument, etc.
- HIGHER THINKING SYSTEM—includes problem solving, logical reasoning, critical and creative thinking, forming and using concepts, and understanding complicated ideas
- SOCIAL THINKING SYSTEM—governs social interaction, working collaboratively, and coping tactfully with others

PUT YOUR CHILD'S NATURAL INTELLIGENCE TO WORK

Since I learned about different intelligences and discovered my own weaknesses, I've made at least feeble attempts to work on them. My nemesis is bodily-kinesthetic intelligence, or the motor system, or a blind spot as to awareness of where my body is in space. Or you could simply just call me a klutz. So I occasionally take classes, hoping they will help. The most recent is tai chi. Today the teacher, a veteran dance instructor, explained how some people are born "knowing" their bodies. The rest, she said, go into other work. I nodded my head in agreement, and gave thanks that people still read books. Then, once again, I shone as the class' negative example (I stand on my heels, don't you know, and that is wrong, wrong, wrong). The child in me wanted to shout, "Yeah, well, I could spell rings around you," but alas, the adult knew the truth: "That doesn't matter here."

If your child possesses intelligences, or learning styles, or superior neurodevelopmental systems unappreciated in the school approach to education, becoming her learning coach could be the greatest gift you ever give her. You can allow her "symptoms" some much-needed time in the sun. This is what customizing your child's learning experience is all about. Help her exercise her favored intelligences and learning styles to follow them as far as she cares to go.

K.I.S.S.: KEEP IT SIMPLE, SILLY!

Learning coaches, it's not only vital to success to customize your child's learning experience, it's equally important to keep the process simple. Only in this way does learning have a chance of becoming part of the natural flow of family life instead of something artificially tacked on to it. Begin with the idea that learning can happen anywhere, any place, any time, with a book or a cloud, and you'll wonder why you didn't do this sooner.

I recently caught up with Lucy, a woman I'd met years ago when we were both learning at home with children of similar ages and, as old friends do, we reminisced about the good old days. As we dined she reminded me of the family event that forced her to simplify learning for her children. When her father got ill, "practically daily we had to take him to appointments, and then after that we visited him in the hospital and nursing home every day. There was no time for planning educational activities, yet the kids kept learning—and well. We carried bags of library books, paper, pens, crayons, and markers, and magnetic letters and words and cookie sheets wherever we went," said Lucy. "We played all kinds of games in the car; hangman, twenty questions, what do you see that begins with b?, roll up the window a quarter of the way, a third of the way. We used the starting and ending odometer readings to practice subtraction in our heads. The kids learned how to use compasses and read maps. To this day I swear Jesse learned to read from road signs. When Dad passed away I vowed to always keep learning as natural—and as simple—as my kids showed me it is, and I never prepared another lesson plan."

It took a family crisis for Lucy to give simple, natural learning a chance. But I've heard her results repeated enough under countless other, more pleasant circumstances enough to know that it works. Not only does it work, the children who are growing and learning what they need to know see it all as fun, not a chore, providing them with a positive perspective on learning.

USING THE THEORY OF
"FLOW" IN YOUR GAME PLAN

For those skeptics out there who still don't believe learning can be fun, let me introduce you to Harvard professor Mihaly Csikezentmihalyi or, as I've come to know him, "Professor C," a friend and colleague of Howard Gardner. In his life's work Professor C. has sought to answer the question, "What makes life worth living?" Much of what he discovered is helpful as we raise and educate children. He calls it the theory of "flow," a metaphor that "describes the sense of effortless action people feel in moments that stand out as the best in their lives." Put this theory to work in your home and you will find customizing your child's learning experience provides him life's best moments, something every loving parent wishes to do.

Flow experiences produce the serenity that comes when heart, will, and mind are on the same page. Three main conditions seem to set the stage for the experience of flow:

- A person faces a clear set of goals that require appropriate responses. Some examples of life activities that make a flow experience likely include golf, mountain climbing, weaving, playing a musical piece; anything that provides the opportunity to focus on clear and compatible goals.

- The activity engaged in provides immediate feedback. How well one is doing in achieving the goal is always extremely obvious; the golfer's ball did or didn't get closer to the hole; the climber slipped or moved higher on the mountain, the last row on the weaver's loom does or doesn't fit the pattern.

- A person's skills are fully involved in overcoming a challenge that is just about manageable. The activity is not so easy as to be boring or so difficult as to cause anxiety.

Remember "curiosity creates interest, interest increases attention to the task at hand, and attention gives rise to learning"? Put a slightly different way in *Finding Flow: The Psychology of Engagement with Everyday Life*, the professor declares that when high challenges are matched with high skills, the result is deep involvement. "Because of the total demand on psychic energy, a person in flow is completely focused. There is no space in consciousness for distracting thoughts . . . When a person's entire being is stretched in the full functioning of body and mind, *whatever* one does becomes worth doing for its own sake; living becomes its own justification. In the harmonious focusing of physical and psychic energy, life finally comes into its own . . . The happiness that follows flow is of our own making, and it leads to increasing complexity and growth in consciousness." (Emphasis added.)

The professor calls flow a magnet for learning, "that is, for developing new levels of challenges and skills. In an ideal situation, a person would be constantly growing while enjoying whatever he or she did." Even at the age of ninety, Linus Pauling, Nobel Prize-winning chemist, "kept the enthusiasm and curiosity of a young child . . . And there was no secret about how he did it; in his own words: 'I just went ahead doing what I liked to do.'"

Professor C. argues that this is not a self-centered indulgence. Indeed, the important point is that "Pauling—and the many others who share his attitude—like to do almost everything, no matter how difficult or trivial, including the things they are forced to do."

Here's one area where your work will have a significant impact on your child's academic career. Without ever focusing on school specifics, such as spelling and science, you can help increase your child's enjoyment of those things he is forced to do in school. This will increase attention to the topics at hand, likely to improve grades.

Learning coaches can erase the definitive lines that separate a math lesson from a needed trip to the grocery store, or a history lesson from the family vacation. And guess what? Highly productive and creative artists, entrepreneurs, statesmen, and scientists tend to experience their jobs in the same way—completely integrated with the rest of their lives.

COACH'S MOTIVATIONAL MINUTE: So often we parents engage in the activities we love, the hobbies and pastimes that provide our own flow experiences, when the kids aren't around. Share what you love with your child. It may not turn out to be of interest to him, but that's okay. He'll have witnessed someone he loves enjoying the pursuit, and experience the pleasure it brings you. At the same time, you'll be getting even better at whatever it is you love to do!

Professor C. says, "One of the most common tropes in the nearly one hundred interviews I conducted with such persons as Nobel Prize winners and other creative leaders in different fields was: 'You could say I worked every minute of my life, or you could say with equal justice that I never worked a day.'"

There is more, so much more, and oh, how I wish I could give each and every reader of this book a copy of *Finding Flow*. Barring this, I can only recommend that you get a copy. It's a cogent argument for learning coaches to encourage your child's "symptoms" through loving attention and acceptance at home. Recognize and encourage his gifts, and even if they're not directly appreciated at school the resulting happiness, increased self-esteem, and pure joy found in doing something for its own sake (as opposed to for a good grade or other recognition) will translate into improved school performance, just as it translates into life improvement in general.

CREATE A LEAN, KEEN LEARNING TEAM

With your learning coach muscles starting to take shape, one additional step is to think of yourself and your child as a team, a lean, keen learning team. I've found many parents consider this aspect of coaching their greatest challenge. At first glance this makes sense. Too many families, pulled in different directions day in and day out, end up living in two different worlds, unable to relate to each other because of it.

Megan remembers all too well how estranged she was beginning to feel from her ten-year old daughter, Kyoko, when she returned home tired from her social work duties each day. "I don't honestly know how it happened, but one day it occurred to me that our relationship could only be termed adversarial," explains Megan, "like I was the enemy prying out confidential information when I tried to talk to Kyoko about friends, school, and her day in general. She considered me 'clueless,' unable to understand so why bother telling me anything."

Fortunately for Megan and Kyoko, the learning coach approach, while helping a child academically, also works to remedy the "two different worlds" situation. Remember preparation includes spending some time and attention increasing trust and respect for a child; this helps the parent see the child as *capable* of being a teammate. Determining a child's weaknesses and strengths in learning helps the parent accept the child as is in order to work *with* him and his natural inclinations instead of being tempted to change them. Discovering how to use this knowledge to create a meaningful learning experience helps the parent put enjoyment of time together first, allowing the learning that naturally occurs to be incidental instead of primary.

Incorporating all of the above into their time together eventually allowed Megan and Kyoko to share the same world at the same time. "I'd never noticed before that when Kyoko and her friends got together they talked a lot about and tried on each other's clothing," remembers Megan. "Then I realized when we watched television she focused less on the plot and more on what everyone was wearing, and she had a very good eye. So I began casually talking to her about clothes; a quick comment about what someone in the grocery store was wearing, a compliment before she raced out the door in the morning on how lovely she looks in pink. Before long she started bringing her magazines into the kitchen while I prepared dinner to talk about the fashions and showed me some of her own sketches I never knew about."

Megan seized the approach of Halloween as an opportunity to work with Kyoko to create her costume. Together they sketched out the attire of a "fashion witch" down to the shoes, then enjoyed several shopping trips searching for the perfect pieces and accessories. "Kyoko didn't just look like a million bucks on Halloween," says

Megan, "she felt like it, too. And like a snowball rolling down a hill, that sense of partnership, once begun, is permeating other areas of life, including talk about friends and schoolwork. We're going to get a sewing machine, too. Think of all the measuring, calculating, budgeting, and creating involved. I can't wait!"

Your child doesn't need to be a budding fashion designer to achieve the team spirit that Megan and Kyoko built. That was just one family's stepping stone toward the emotional and psychological support that creates an environment conducive to connection, sharing and, most importantly, caring about each other. We can take a page from the business coach's handbook and develop the behavior—in ourselves and our children—supportive of teamwork:

- Watch for or create opportunities to blend your individual talents together to accomplish something neither of you would be able to accomplish individually

- Provide true help when asked, such as spelling the word instead of telling the child to go look it up, and offer assistance without being asked

- Share all kinds of information and welcome each other into activities

Megan and Kyoko's success underscores the importance of three aspects of teamwork readily available to you and your child in your home.

CONVERSING

The first and most important way to build a learning team is the unfortunately nearly extinct art of conversation, but it becomes possible when families make the effort to create time together. As Megan's example illustrates, conversation about any topic under the sun—not just school work—helps both parties better understand each other. Feel pressed for time? Here are some ideas to help you stretch the time you have for conversation, and create a little more. Consider starting with the ideas that best blend into your family's existing routine, or come up with even more ideas of your own.

- *Use a slow-cooker.* Spend a few minutes in the morning getting the ingredients into the cooker and return home to dinner well on its way to being ready.

- *Dine together.* It may sound old-fashioned, and it may take a little time for everyone to get into the habit, but it works.

- *While in the car together turn off the radio.* (I once bought a car for little other reason than it didn't even have a radio—the salesman, I'm sure, was delighted to be rid of it.) Use this time to talk, about anything under the sun.

- *Schedule regular family nights.* Learning coaches have nights just for board games, watching movies, playing music, dancing, exercising, inventing, arts and crafts, letter writing, creative writing, jigsaw puzzles, ethnic cooking, and reading. What does your family like to do?

- *Create family night out.* Even the smallest communities offer family-centered activities many of us don't take advantage of. Talks and demonstrations on subjects of interest, plays, musical performances, church suppers, strawberry picking, movies, bowling, festivals, history days, roller skating, ice skating, miniature golf, viewing neighborhood Christmas lights . . . You'd probably never have to do the same activity twice.

- *Plan vacations with conversation in mind.* Long car trips anywhere, camping, hiking, the beach, touring museums and historical sites, visiting relatives, anything that provides a bit of time away from perpetual motion.

- *Perform household chores together.* Where is it written that Mom should be the only one having fun cooking, cleaning, doing dishes, and laundry? Gathering and loading laundry into the washer may only provide a few minutes together, but those are a few more minutes than you would have otherwise.

- *Utilize bedtime.* Rare is the child with an 8 PM bedtime who is fast asleep at 8:05 PM. Learning coaches find this is a nice time to unwind with their children, read a little, talk about the day just past or plan for tomorrow. Families find this generally increases conversation time by ten to thirty minutes.

- *Invite a dinner guest.* Whether it's Aunt Mabel, the senior citizen next door, or your pet's veterinarian, dinner guests stimulate conversation and punctuate it with a different perspective.

- *Become early birds.* If you and/or your child prefer the sound of morning larks to night owls, set your alarms to rise a bit earlier than usual, even if only on a couple of mornings each week. Treat yourselves with a special breakfast together.

- *Stretch your weekends.* You'll already be doing this to some degree when you get in the habit of including your child in household chores like laundry. On weekends you can extend that to yard work, gardening, household maintenance, shopping at the grocery store or Home Depot, or giving the dog a bath.

- *Give your activity calendar a spring cleaning.* Your child is only young once, and I can attest to the fact you will have a lot more time for yourself in what seems the blink of an eye. So in the meantime, consider whether any of your current activities can wait until your child doesn't require as much of your time and attention. Think hard before taking on new responsibilities out-side the home, no matter how worthy the cause (charity really does begin at home). Figure out if some of your family's daily or weekly activities can be consolidated by changing the time or day at which they occur. Pick up a book on time management — they sell well because you're not the only person looking to maximize the potential of every day.

STIMULATING CONVERSATION WITH YOUR TEAMMATE

Learning coaches employ a variety of ways to stimulate conversation with their children that leads to bonding—and learning! Try some of these at dinnertime, or anytime, choosing age-appropriate topics, and grabbing opportunities to help your child reach to understand. As with conversation with your peers, you'll find yourselves heading off in wonderful, unforeseen directions.

DISCUSS NEWS TOPICS EVERYONE IS FAMILIAR WITH:
- Trials
- New movies
- Sports stars' salaries
- Performance of sports teams and upcoming games
- Wars
- Political races
- The newest best seller in children's literature
- Latest scientific discoveries
- The proposed new mall
- The latest video game or toy
- Local ecological challenges

ASK SOME OF THE "BIG" QUESTIONS:
- What are the important things in life?
- What do you do best? In what jobs do people often get to do that?

- What existing world problem is most important to fix? How might we do this?
- Is the space program important? Why or why not?
- Do you intend to get married? Have children? How many?
- Where would you like to live when you grow up?
- What do you think you'll have in your home when you're an adult that we don't have now?
- What is meant by the saying, "(fill in a common quote, proverb, saying)?"
- What might each of us be able to do to keep the house a little neater?

ASK SOME QUESTIONS JUST FOR FUN:
- What do you suppose is the (longest, shortest, heaviest, lightest) (animal, plant, planet, fish, person) in the world? How will we find out?
- Where did the (any item in your home) come from? Where did its use originate?
- If you could have dinner with a famous (artist, inventor, president, sports hero, musician) past or present, who would you choose? What would you talk about?
- If we went on a trip to (fill in a place), what would you pack? Why?
- How might you rewrite the end of (insert name of favorite movie or book)?
- If you could live on another planet, which one would it be? Why?
- If you had to be a bug, which would you be?

COLLABORATING

The dictionary defines collaborate as "to work together, especially in a joint intellectual effort." As a budding learning coach, Megan adeptly built team spirit by collaborating with Kyoko. Marta discovered, "As a working mom, my eight-year old daughter, Ava, and I have found our collaborative efforts the most time effective as a learning team. We typically discuss and choose from short-term projects, like performing a survey for the U.S. Geological Survey's *Frogwatch USA*, or projects that can be completed piecemeal, like the history timeline hanging in our living room. This way," Marta points out, "we're actually physically working together, unlike when she does homework by herself and I just check it over after the fact."

MODELING THINKING PROCESSES

In addition to increasing conversation and saving time, collaboration gives you a chance to model adult thought processes. With all that teachers try to cover in the classroom, rarely do they demonstrate for children *how to think*. Since showing children *how* to think is much more important than telling them *what* to think, as learning coach you can engage in a remarkably simple and effective method I call "thinking out loud." It's exercise for the brain, building the muscle your child needs for thinking, reasoning, analyzing, problem solving, and even daydreaming.

"At first I felt a little silly thinking out loud, but I couldn't deny it was working when one day I responded to a radio news report and my daughter, Carla, asked why I said that," says Tara, a state police dispatcher and mom to a toddler as well as six-year-old Carla. "We actually talked about the reasons to close a landfill for ten minutes!"

Tara continues thinking out loud while around Carla. "It might be better to invite Grandpa to dinner Friday night instead of Sunday night." "Should we go pick up the dry cleaning and then go to the grocery store, or the other way around?" "Do you think I should heat up six rolls or eight? How many do you think everyone will want?"

Tara swears she can "see Carla's wheels turning" as she considers her mother's verbal musings. "She considers that Grandpa has to get up for work on Monday so he can stay later if he comes on Friday," says Tara. "She figures out that going to the grocery store first means we'll pass the ice cream store on the way home from the dry cleaners. She's totally concentrated while mentally calculating how many rolls four of us will eat. I've noticed she now offers her opinion more frequently, and thinks through the consequences of decisions before making them. Her teacher remarked on her relative maturity at a recent parent-teacher conference. I haven't felt silly about thinking out loud since."

I hope you'll find collaborating with your child and thinking out loud as rewarding as the learning coaches who report they feel their own curiosity and imagination waking up in the process.

LAUGHING + LOVING = LEARNING

As the mother of an eleven-year-old son diagnosed with Attention Deficit Disorder, Wanda knew all too well what it was like trying the traditional method of helping her eight-year-old son Adam every evening, who was constantly falling behind in schoolwork. "Frustrating is the only word to describe it," she says, "for both of us. I'd make him sit straight at the dining room table as I reread every single lesson in every single subject to him. Within five minutes he'd be crawling under the table, or drumming on the table, or watching a housefly's flight path. I'd regain his attention, I'd lose it again, and we repeated this over and over. No matter how long we sat there, he couldn't answer the simplest questions about the material immediately after we went over it."

One beautiful sunny afternoon Adam was jumping on his backyard trampoline when Wanda called him in for lessons. Adam dawdled, and Wanda decided she would like to get some sun, so she took the books outside. "I was going to make him sit with me at the picnic table, but instead I just pulled up a lawn chair next to the trampoline and started reading from his science book as he laughed and jumped," she remembers. "I asked the first review question and he got it right. Then he got the next and the next. I was so excited I started jumping up and down on the ground right along with him and he said, 'Hey, Mom, we should do this all the time. It's fun!'"

Fortunately for those who live in apartments and condos or who have small backyards, not every child requires a trampoline to learn. But every child can learn better and faster when love and laughter enter the equation. When your understanding of education moves from the need to teach to rekindling and facilitating the natural compulsion to learn, it grows clearer every day that to live is to learn. We do children a grave injustice when we perpetuate the separation of the two that tends to make it harder, not easier, to learn and enjoy it.

Learning for all, but especially young children, should be just as full of love and laughter as life itself, knocking down the barriers that lead children to believe learning is difficult, boring, a burden, a chore. The best thing about love and laughter is that they are unique to you and your child, and you can put your own spin on them. Just as Wanda and Adam did, you can draw them from every day life, from things you would do anyway. Does your child collect Beanie Babies, or teddy bears, or dinosaurs? Let them read with you, too, in their own voices and personalities. Does your child adore Harry Potter? Include Harry in conversations about everything from adding to spelling. Join your child as he exercises and builds imagination and creativity, be it in story form, art, or playing with toys. Don't be afraid to be silly; children love it and it keeps you young. Your newfound enjoyment of learning will translate into school performance improvement, as a warm environment inspires learning that sticks.

CHAPTER 5

THE SIX HABITS OF SUCCESSFUL LEARNERS

Tannika, mom of two young boys with the biggest brown eyes you've ever seen, caught my attention during a short break in a learning coach workshop she was attending; I sat next to her to talk.

"I'm wondering," she said, "just who thought school was a good idea. It seems to me that sitting at a desk in school and jumping from subject to subject, just may be the absolutely worst way to expect a kid to learn things!"

Tannika realized how the sit-still-and-listen method of teaching goes against the grain of how human beings actually learn after our workshop group briefly visited the fascinating topic, just as you and I will do in this chapter. Armed with this knowledge, it's easier for Tannika and other learning coaches to inspire their children to acquire the six habits of successful learners. Remember, weave a thread of it everyday, and at last we cannot break it. It works the same way for your child.

By the end of this chapter you'll see why learning coaches often recognize that one of the greatest rewards of their "work" is that it becomes an integral aspect of their children's lives. The fruit of their labor truly lasts a lifetime. Once a child learns how to learn—in other words once he truly becomes a learner—that awareness remains forever. No one can ever take it away from him.

When it comes to success in school, the studies and surveys reported in the news often credit indicators such as socio-economic status, membership in a nuclear family, and/or specific ethnic backgrounds. Over the years I've chatted with and interviewed countless young learners, paying special attention to the most successful among them. While the reported criteria may apply across the board in a most generic fashion, or to success in school (which in many cases is not the same as successful learning), these criteria haven't been borne out in my own unscientific research. Successful learners live in all socio-economic conditions, every conceivable family arrangement and, of course, they span the spectrum of the world's ethnicities.

Those who find themselves at the top of the student success scale share much more meaningful criteria that, unfortunately for researchers, is not easily measured by numbers and surveys. Patterns in their feelings about and practices in learning have been supported by a caring adult as they grow. These patterns and practices have become the habits of their success. Check out which ones are already wonderful habits for your child and which it would be helpful to encourage her to build.

HIP, HIP, HOORAY!
(SETS AND CELEBRATES GOALS)

It's repeated practically every day in every school with every child. The goal is a good test score, period. But even for those students who accomplish the goal, the good test score is merely added to an ever-growing string of grades to be averaged for a report card. The next test is only days—or even hours—away, and so the achieved goal is quickly forgotten. (This, of course, does not address the question of whether the same information, retained long enough to receive a good test score, has truly become part of the child's knowledge base.)

One of the very first steps that life, business, and career coaches take to help their adult clients achieve success is a crash course in goal-setting. Children can quickly see the value, too, when you employ the analogy of creating a map that shows how to get where he wants to go. In this way he learns the importance of goals, planning, and preparing. It's never too early to acclimate your child to the idea of setting, achieving, and celebrating goals.

Yolanda, a single mom, knew that while his school performance wasn't stellar, her rambunctious, precocious only child, ten-year old Miguel, was smart. "Goal orientation seemed like a way he could focus his attention and energy," Yolanda says, "but we had to start small."

Yolanda was smart. She called it "starting small." We'll call it beginning with short-term goals. To a young child, three weeks may as well be light-years away, so goals must be achievable in time frames he can wrap his mind around to avoid frustration. They should be measured in terms of hours and days, a week at most, and grow longer termed as the child matures.

"I told Miguel that I wanted to try a new pet store but didn't know where it was, and asked him to help me plan the route on a local real estate map I picked up for that purpose," Yolanda says. "With our mission accomplished, I explained how the map helped us take the best, most direct route possible, and that maybe we could have some fun doing the same with his school nemesis, totally illegible handwriting."

"'Like a map for writing?' he asked me. All of a sudden he was excited about writing, but," Yolanda adds with a smile, "it had to *literally* be a map, so I bought two bright green (Miguel's favorite color) poster boards and stapled them together. We discussed the final destination (the goal), and he liked 'write a paper in cursive and my teacher can read every word.' We put that at the top right of the map, then back-tracked to the lower left of the map to start the route we'd take to get there."

Yolanda and Miguel brainstormed for days, keeping a list of potential "landmarks" for the boy's writing map. Yolanda began the "trip" with several easier goals, such as forming single troublesome letters, then interspersed a few easy goals with harder ones, such as whole words containing letters that were most difficult for Miguel. After six weeks of traveling his word highway, Miguel reached the final destination, on which his teacher, aware of Yolanda's efforts, wrote, "Bravo, Miguel! I can read every word!"

The next evening dinner concluded with a carrot cake decorated with the teacher's quote. "I also gift-wrapped a hardcover journal and gave it to Miguel that night, telling him that since he can now read everything he writes he might want to keep special writings in his own book," Yolanda adds. "He began practicing his handwriting *and* creating his own little stories in that journal all on his own—in less than two months."

Just as it did for Miguel, establishing, meeting, and celebrating goals eases children into the habit of increased responsibility for their own education. Because they often do things like write, read, add, and subtract because they *have to*, pursuing such things because they *want to* often doesn't occur to them. As learning coach you can add meaning—which opens the door to enjoyment—by introducing your child to the power of goal setting and its inherent rewards.

JUST BECAUSE
(READS FOR PLEASURE AND INFORMATION)

Since 1992 the National Assessment of Educational Progress (NAEP) issues what many call "the nation's report card." According to a report from the Heartland Institute, in 2000 "almost four of every ten American fourth-graders (37 percent) scored 'below basic,' meaning they were unable to read after completing their K-3 instruction. For the past eight years, average reading scores have not budged off dreadful. Poor and minority children have fallen even further behind, despite billions in Title 1 spending to push them forward."

Then Secretary of Education Roderick R. Paige declared, "After spending $125 billion of Title 1 money over twenty-five years we have virtually nothing to show for it."

In 2003, *The Washington Post* summarized reading scores by stating: "The results showed that 36 percent of fourth-graders and 25 percent of eighth-graders performed below the basic level, failing to demonstrate even partial mastery of reading . . . reading scores were uniformly disappointing among the nation's high school seniors, with 26 percent scoring below basic in 2002."

Now, I'll admit I'm a mother who, although I felt pretty silly doing it, read to all three of my children en utero. As a homeschooling mother, I also taught all three how to read. I don't remember exactly how the deed was accomplished, but I know we used the Ball-Stick-Bird book series for the ten-or-so-minutes per day of "formal" instruction. We spent much more time reading aloud (first just me, then each of them as they were able), and carting bagsful of books home from the library (their choices as well as mine). They watched me read for various purposes constantly, and I observed which types of materials best lit their learning fires (one loved the Hardy Boys, another the Little House on the Prairie series, and another poured over *National Geographic* magazines). I read aloud just as many adult books as children's. I remember that during read-alouds the youngest always first got comfortable on the floor, using our dog, good ol' Bandit, as a pillow while covering himself (head included) with the afghan that was ever-available on the couch. There were relatively few tears (on their parts or mine).

This approach to reading, if one can even call it an approach (it was more like "Let's see if this works," and what worked was a little different with each child), is similar to the informal, holistic, painless way many homeschooling parents find successful with children. It flies in the face of the commonly accepted practice of dissecting reading into daily lessons that produce the abysmal test scores previously noted. But the worst part is, dissection can turn kids off to reading anything they don't *have* to read.

Successful learners *enjoy* reading. When their curiosity is piqued about something, they don't mind reading what's necessary to find out more and so experience a utilitarian reason for doing it. They also read for pleasure. Not only does this continually sharpen their skill, it also:

- Exercises imagination
- Increases curiosity
- Builds vocabulary
- Exposes them to proper spelling
- Exposes different forms of writing as well as personal styles
- Increases ability to be communicated to

As O. Prescott wrote in *A Father Reads to His Child*, "Few children learn to love books themselves. Someone must lure them into the wonderful world of the written word, someone must show them the way." An article written by Robert O. Fisch, M.D., Marty Smith, M.A., and Margaret Yatsevitch Phinney, Ed. D. for the *American Family Physician* points out four pivotal factors that create a positive environment for learning to read:

- Opportunity for exposure—the availability of printed materials (not only books)

- Modeling—the presence of others who demonstrate that they value reading by engaging in it daily

- Opportunity for engagement—an environment that facilitates contact with paper and pencil and experimentation with writing

- Supportive feedback—positive responses to children's experimentations with storytelling and "writing," support of their conversations, answers to their questions, and encouragement to reconstruct favorite stories from memory

As a learning coach, you can add lots of talk, storytelling, and reading aloud for a winning combination. This is true no matter your child's age. Don't stop when your child becomes a proficient reader. When you read, discuss, and share stories you build a warehouse of common experience. This provides lots of opportunities to discuss matters big and small, find common interests, get to know each other better, and strengthen family bonds, not to mention enjoying fine literature in the process.

LEARNING . . . WHAT IS IT GOOD FOR? (UNDERSTANDS UTILITY)

Homework time was headache time in Tammy's home. With nine year-old triplets, all boys, "I thought if I heard 'Why do I have to learn this stuff?' one more time I would pull out every hair on my head," says Tammy.

She works in the human resources department of a large corporation, so I asked her, "What if you went into work one day and your boss gave you an assignment to which you could see no connection to your job? Even better, what if he asked you to do the assignment over and over again? How many times do you think you'd repeat it before asking him why you're doing this?"

"Once," said Tammy, smiling before she added, "maybe."

Human nature dictates that there is a motivation, a purpose, in exchange for our energy. Without this motivation, CIAL doesn't have a chance to blossom, let alone unfold, in students or workers. Successful learners can see a reason for, and therefore understand, the utility of learning, thus the energy needed to accomplish the task flows easier, with much less resistance, which leads to ever greater success.

Due to the large number of children and small amount of time in a classroom situation, it's difficult to provide the necessary under-standing of utility. Tammy decided that when next a complaint echoed through the house, she would see what happened if she spent a week focusing on helping her boys see how their efforts benefit them.

She didn't wait long. The next evening Tim complained about what to him looked like an endless list of spelling words. "I told the boys I was really busy and would need their help this week. Then I included them in all the day-to-day writing." says Tammy. "When something needed to be added to the grocery list, a note left for the UPS man about an expected delivery, or a check written, I asked one of them to do it. I had them answer the phone and take mes-sages, create my daily to-do lists, and fill out a couple of on-line order forms."

Before the week was over the house was filled with a different kind of hollering: "Hey, Mom, how do you spell package?" "Tim, is there an *e* or an *a* in mustard?" "Hey, I took a message from Mr. Gooseman; now that's a funny name!"

"I kid you not," Tammy told me. "You could have knocked me over with a feather when Tim said, 'Boy, you write a *lot*. No wonder we need to learn how to spell so many words."

At this point Tammy sat them all down in the living room just before dinner. They were ready for the message. "This week,"

Tammy told them, "you saw how it can benefit you to learn how to spell all those words on your lists. When you grow up you have to write all the time! You can do it faster when you know how to spell the words. And," Tammy added, "I'll be honest with you boys. You know I work in the department responsible for hiring new employees. Job applications and resumes full of misspelled words make us wonder if the person will pay attention to the many details of the job, or if he or she can communicate effectively with other employees or the public in general because that's a big part of the job."

Once Tammy's boys saw the frequently reinforced answer to "what's in it for me?" the complaints dwindled, then disappeared. The complaints about spelling disappeared, anyway. When last I spoke with Tammy they were having fun working on the importance of geographical awareness.

LIKE A FIDDLE (STAYS FIT)

Every child is an individual because she is a unique blend of the physical, mental, emotional and, many would add, the spiritual. Successful learners are not simply walking intellects, but rather a complicated blend of all of the above. As learning coach you can see to it that every aspect, what in the seventies was commonly referred to as "the whole child," is nourished and in shape.

Let's Get Physical

A healthy physical condition may be more important to successful learners than ten hours of homework each night. Because there are no firm lines between the different aspects of human beings, a healthy body contributes to the well-being of the mental, emotional, and spiritual aspects, and vice-versa. Learning coaches can focus on three major areas to help their children stay physically strong. (And don't forget the benefits of each for you, too!)

NUTRITION

Children are works of art in progress. We can look at the family clothing bill and see they are getting taller and their feet are growing by leaps and bounds, but internal growth occurs at the same time. Nutritious input builds healthy eyes, bones, muscles, and internal organs.

Debbie, a part-time legal secretary, made the connection between nutrition and learning when by chance she delivered a book to her nine year old daughter's school at lunchtime. "I couldn't distinguish exactly what the smell that permeated every hallway was," says Debbie, "but I knew immediately why Sherry constantly complained about lunch. I peeked into the cafeteria and there she was eating cookies and a bag of potato chips, just like the majority of kids around her."

When Mom and daughter returned home that afternoon Debbie learned that Sherry hadn't purchased a "real" lunch all year, and neither did any of the "cool kids." Before falling asleep that night, Debbie made a note of the several subject areas Sherry was having trouble with. Debbie's intuition was right; every one of them was addressed in the afternoon, at which time, thanks to the lunch, Sherry's energy quickly peaked then took a nose dive.

"I realized I wasn't exactly the world's greatest eating role model, either," Debbie admits, "so I started changing the diet for all of us, including my husband, immediately. Before my focus was on convenience, now it's on nutrition."

Debbie shares some of the positive changes her family made:

- Don't skip breakfast or eat it on the run
- Keep a regular schedule for all meals, including dinner
- Eat at the table together, not in front of the television or separately in different rooms
- Prepare the next day's healthy, hand-packed lunch (no more cafeteria food!) together just before the child's bedtime
- Instead of frying, think bake, broil, roast, or poach
- Don't argue over eating; researchers claim it can take up to ten introductions of a new food before children get comfortable with it
- Try five small meals per day, or a couple of snacks in-between reduced "regular" meals
- Limit, but don't forbid, small or occasional treats

"It took a while for all of us to get into the habit of taking—and appreciating—healthier meals and snacks, but after six months we adjusted quite nicely," says Debbie. "We combined this with more family exercise, and I saw a slow but steady change in Sherry's energy level which eventually translated into better grades in those afternoon classes. Now," adds Debbie, "she still has to smell the cafeteria lunch, but she doesn't eat junk to avoid it."

HEALTHY SNACK SUGGESTIONS

- Pretzels
- Dried fruit
- Air-popped popcorn (with salt-free seasoning)
- Whole grain crackers or rice cakes topped with low-fat cheese, peanut butter, soy nut butter, fruit spread
- Fruits and nuts
- Cereals with no- or low-fat milk
- "Parfaits" of low-fat yogurt, fruit, and granola cereal
- Fruit Smoothies of low-fat milk or yogurt blended with fresh or frozen fruit

EXERCISE

As Debbie noted, exercise is a second prong of physical fitness that maximizes the benefits of good nutrition. While most children participate in what are known as physical education (PE) classes, a 2003 study by the National Institute of Child Health and Human Development (NICHD) discovered that, on average, children had 2.1 PE classes per week. "For each class," notes a National Institutes of Health press release, "students engaged in only about 4.8 minutes of vigorous physical activity." Successful learners need more than ten minutes per week to stay in shape.

"We cut back drastically on television, video games, and computer time," says Debbie, "and replaced them with long, or at least fast, walks, bicycling, jump roping, rollerblading, crazy fast dancing, and aerobic exercise in the living room and, Sherry's favorite, playing basketball. We simply encourage her to do *something* physical each day, and since she enjoys a variety of activity, it's relatively easy. My husband and I knew we had to be role models here, too, so we rekindled our love of hiking and try to incorporate at least one fun exercise-filled activity each weekend. You'd be surprised how much you walk while visiting the zoo or chasing the dog around the park!"

AVOID OBESITY

While everyone knows too much fast food, soda, and candy are loaded with calories, research suggests that when it comes to your child, too much television, viewing's subsequent lack of exercise, and the habit of snacking while watching, are much more harmful. Playing video games isn't quite as bad, as even minor motor movements burn up energy and increases metabolic rate.

A Mathematica Policy Research, Inc. study found that "one-third of all children under two years of age consume virtually no fruits or vegetables." Dr. William Dietz, director of the Division of Nutrition and Physical Activity in the Center for Chronic Disease Prevention and Health Promotion at the Centers for Disease Control and Prevention, cautions that parents, "not children, need to be in charge of what food is served at mealtime, and children can choose whether to eat it or not."

As both a parent and learning coach you don't want to starve your child for fear of obesity, so how much food is "enough?" Interestingly, it depends on your child's age. "A three and a half-year old," says Dr. Dietz, "will generally eat the same amount of food whether he's given a large or small portion. At age five, however, the amount of food consumed increases when portion size does." He recommends that a good mealtime strategy, then, is "to put a little food on a child's plate, rather than loading it up, and let the child ask for more if he wants it."

Mentally Fit

Just as an unused muscle gets weak and flabby so, too, does a brain when it doesn't receive enough exercise. For success in school and life, make brain workouts fun and interesting so your child looks forward to them and gets in the habit of pursuing such exercise on his own.

It's important to pump up logic, attention, language, visual skills, and memory—short-term, long-term, and a lesser discussed memory especially important to children in school called "working memory." While short-term memory holds information for seconds, and long-term memory permanently stores processed information, we can think of working memory as somewhere in between. In the 1980's, English researchers Baddeley and Hitch named it "working memory" because of its ability to hold several facts in memory temporarily while performing an unrelated task or solving a problem. (Think about the last time you kept repeating a phone number until you found a piece of paper, or repeating directions as you kept driving—that's working memory.)

Because it's used to understand spoken language, comprehend reading, write stories, and perform some math operations, it's important that your child's working memory gets frequent workouts. Researchers call the exercise "maintenance rehearsal," but as learning coach you surely can make it a lot more fun than that sounds. They also note that while the practice is pretty self-evident to adults, it's something we learned along the way. Five year-olds, researchers claim, rarely practice the strategy on their own, while the habit is more common, though not universal, among ten year-olds.

Be sure to play any or all of the available board games that offer exercise, but you can utilize your travel time or afternoon at the beach, too. With younger children, you can start with a simple series of letters. You say "l," your child says "l." You add "z," and your child says, "l, z," and so on. You can do the same with objects—bear, tree, book, rice, etc. Play "Goin' on a Bear Hunt." As the child gets older, add the challenge of taking things on the bear hunt in alphabetical order. You can make your own "Memory" game with index cards, putting the same letter, number, word, or picture on two cards. Shuffle them, place them face-down on a table, and take turns making matches. You can start with 10 to 12 cards for the youngest children, then add more as rate of success increases.

Assignments around the house make great practice, too. "When my children, Dylan and Danielle, were about four years-old, I started giving them short lists of simple things to do," explains learning coach Jen, "like comb your hair, pick up your books, and turn off the TV. I was surprised at how easily they always forgot the second two things! But the more we did it, the better they got," she says, "and now at ages seven and nine, they enjoy the challenge of trying to remember six or seven verbal instructions. Hmm," Jen adds, "I should probably do this with my husband, too."

MAKING MAINTENANCE REHEARSAL FUN

Did you know that many popular board games offer painless, fun, maintenance rehearsal? Try these:

- Battleship
- Risk
- Clue
- Mancala
- Connect Four
- Tic Tac Twice
- Royal Masquerade
- Gobblet
- Quick Backgammon and Chess
- Secret Square
- Simon and Bop
- The Memory Game

Emotionally Fit

It's hard to think, let alone learn, when emotional turmoil brews inside. Many events upset a child and, depending on age, it can be difficult for her to express in words what's going on inside. Without this acceptable way to seek understanding she may "act out;" become sullen or rebellious, cry easily or refuse to display any emotion, stop eating or eat far too much. The source could be as significant as the death of a loved one, separation or divorce of parents, or a best friend moving away. It could be as seemingly inconsequential as being called dumb (or smart) by a classmate, unease about an upcoming trip, or trouble grasping a new concept in class. Or, the source could be the typical trials and tribulations that make a youngster feel less secure as she grows more independent.

SOMEONE TO WATCH OVER ME

The simplest and most effective way to ensure your child's mind and heart are clear to focus when necessary is to provide a secure emotional foundation. That foundation consists of the trust and acceptance in relationship with you, and the warmth and security of the environment he calls home.

Within this framework and with your empathy and support he can learn to share his feelings while enjoying the freedom to "vent." Lots of conversation helps, especially within the relaxed environment of play where stuffed animals or dolls might more easily express what's on his mind. Paraphrase or summarize what it is you believe he is telling you. At the same time, this assures him that someone is listening and cares, it also helps him learn how to articulate feelings with words instead of attitudes that turn your household upside down.

SLEEP

Did your mother ever tell you about the value of a good night's sleep? Today's researchers back her up, stating in an October, 2004, *Health Day News* article that it does, indeed, help improve a child's recall. While conducting two different studies—one on motor skills and the other on speech memory—researchers found "participants performed better after sleeping in both." In fact, the author of one of the studies, Matthew Walker, an instructor of psychiatry at Harvard Medical School, states, "It's almost as though at night an editor comes in while you're sleeping and reorganizes and enhances our memories to prepare them for the next day." He further claims that the last two hours of sleep in an eight-hour night are the most critical for memory storage.

Just at the time your child hits puberty and is biologically "hard-wired" to stay up late, is when he actually needs more sleep! While the average teen sleeps 7.3 hours, "research at the National Center on Sleep Disorders at the National Institutes of Health (NIH), shows that children who regularly sleep nine hours perform better in school, are happier, suffer fewer accidents, and are less likely to develop weight or emotional problems later on than those who try to function on less."

Because their internal clocks put them on a different sleep cycle, older children should still be sleeping when school schedules often begin. As additional extra-curricular activities and homework loads often provide reasons to extend the day by staying up later, teenagers are the children who suffer most, along with their grades, from bad sleep habits. There will be more rest for the weary, yourself included, if you help your child form good sleep habits as early as possible.

Children sleep best when they go to bed and wake at the same time every day (this includes weekends and holidays). Once again, your growing observation skills can come in handy. Experts suggest you can set a good, individualized bedtime for your child by putting him to bed at the same time every night for one week, then tracking what time he awakens. The average amount of sleep is a good indicator of just how much sleep your little individual needs.

Ideally, the bedroom should be cool and pre-bedtime should be as calm and relaxing as possible. (While children need a lot of exercise, just before bed is not the right time. Discontinue any heavy exercise at least three hours prior to bedtime.) Bedtime rituals contribute to a sense of calm. This is a great time for your child to shower or bathe, then to read together, listen to music, chat quietly, and snuggle.

Researchers recommend cutting caffeine completely, or at the very least after 2 PM. A chocolate candy bar contains six mg. of caffeine, some sodas and sports drinks as much as 23 mg., and a tiny little scoop of coffee ice cream provides its lucky recipient with 58 mg.!

Equally important to dietary and exercise concerns related to sleep, you can coach your child to success by instilling reasonable, intelligent time-management skills. While as a ten-year-old he does-n't yet have a life-altering exam to take or paper to prepare, some day he will. And he'll be much better prepared to handle inevitable time crunches when you take the time now to help him understand about setting regular schedules in which to accomplish important work. A personal planner, available at any office supply store, pro-vides visual enforcement of "where the time goes."

WHAT A DAY FOR A DAYDREAM
(HAS ADEQUATE "DOWN TIME")

Just the other day a dear friend and business associate sent an email asking, "Linda, when was the last time you felt bored?" Both he and I marveled at the fact that not only couldn't we remember, we didn't foresee another day of boredom ever! At least my friend and I had at one time experienced days of nowhere to go, nothing to do. Research of 3500 children ages twelve and under, from the University of Michigan Institute for Social Research, reveals that children today have half as much free time as those who romped thirty years ago.

Maybe it's because there are so many more organized activities for children today. Parental zeal to create a well-rounded child with many talents means that we can't imagine letting any opportunity pass by. Throw in the all-American ideal that we have to make every minute count, and soon we're tired and stressed parents raising children from behind the driver's seat of the car who can't remember what our backyards look like.

Believe it or not, successful learners know that downtime is full—full of benefits, that is, and they and their families go out of their way to make sure they get it. It's so important that when a child leaves school to learn at home, it's recommended that a parent provide what has come to be known as "decompression time." To decompress means "to relieve of pressure," and that's exactly what downtime does for your child. Pressure created by school attendance comes from many directions and may be subtle or blatant. It's quite possible that a child isn't even aware that the pressure exists because he hardly remembers anything different. Think about the way addiction to caffeine, nicotine, and alcohol occur. The effects of pressure sneak up like that.

Adele was once the consummate soccer mom to two healthy boys, now ages 10 and 13. "There wasn't a sport they didn't play, a Scout activity they missed, and I never heard of an 'enrichment' class I didn't fall in love with," Adele explains. "Then fortunately I read a book called *Einstein Never Used Flashcards: How Our Children Really Learn and Why They Need to Play More and Memorize Less*. It talked about how kids need time to recharge their batteries as well as to process all the information they take in. That made sense to me."

Adele's family performed a schedule overhaul that included putting the televisions in boxes in the garage to be taken out only to watch a specific show and put back again. At first the boys felt deprived and complained they were bored, but Adele patiently suggested activities, participated when she could, and allowed them the opportunity to feel boredom. It only took about six months for everyone to grow more comfortable with the free time—and for the boys to figure out how to fill it themselves.

"Over the last few years they've seen and explored much they would have missed if we'd kept running at the pace we were at," explains Adele. "They've tracked animals, watched a Monarch butterfly develop; right now they're building a fort out back. Their creativity improved, too, because one would say to the other, 'Hey, let's make a new board game,' or 'let's make some instruments and start a band.' They started reading for pleasure more, too," she adds.

Adele couldn't see what was also going on *inside* the boys during their downtime. Receiving information and facts is only one part of the learning process. Equally important is the time to think about that information, allow those neurons to make connections, turn the information inside out and upside down and see what happens, and apply it in meaningful ways. Downtime provides time to apply information over and over again. It's the practice that makes perfect.

"There's a myth that doing nothing is wasting time when it's actually extremely productive and essential," says Dr. Hirsch-Pasek. "During empty hours kids explore the world at the own pace, develop their own unique set of interests, and indulge in the sort of fantasy play that will help them figure out how to create their own happiness, handle problems with others on their own, and sensibly manage their own time. That's a critical life skill."

Downtime is also time for unorganized play, the time when kids are kids. This is where children learn simple but valuable social skills, like taking turns and sharing. They learn the skills of tolerating situations that don't go the way they'd prefer, and making mistakes. Play nourishes imagination and creativity, skills every successful learner needs in the classroom and throughout life. The next time you hear your child say, "I'm bored," smile and think about all the promise that little phrase holds.

DOES YOUR CHILD KNOW HOW TO PLAY?

- Hide and Go Seek
- Tag
- Dodge Ball
- Hot and Cold (getting closer or farther away from a chosen object)
- Store or Post Office
- Pick-up Sticks
- Jacks
- Twenty Questions
- Catch or Frisbee

USE IT OR LOSE IT
(EXPERIENCES AND EXPERIMENTS)

We're all guilty of having done it at some point in our academic careers. We crammed a chapter or a course-ful of information into our heads for no other reason than so we could regurgitate it as answers to test questions. When it was all over we weren't yet out the classroom door when the information drained out, just as if our brains were sieves. Can we (or anyone) honestly say we "learned" that material?

There's a relatively easy test to answer this question—did the information "stick"? If need be, could we draw upon it today? If someone gave you a quadratic equation right now, could you solve it? If asked to explain the chemical reason why baking soda mixed with vinegar becomes a bubbly mess, could you? I couldn't; and anyone I've ever asked who doesn't use such information every day has never said he could, either. Ah, "anyone who doesn't use it every day." Could this be the key?

As successful learners will testify, it certainly is. And as your child's learning coach, you don't concentrate on giving him more information. Instead, you provide lots of opportunity to use the information he is already receiving. The easiest and most effective way to do this is through providing lots of opportunity for experience and experimentation, just as Trish did for her very successful learner, Robert, age twelve.

"I looked at my job of learning coach more as reinforcement than teaching," explains Trish. "I'd look at what he was doing in school, then look at what was around the house and where we could go or who we could speak with, to try to come up with ways he could actually put that information to work." Trish used many of the tried-and-true methods. In the early years, Robert counted silverware as he removed it from the dishwasher; learned about sorting and colors by helping with laundry; learned to tell time on a pocket watch bequeathed to him by a grandfather. As he grew, "use it or lose it" grew right along with him.

"When Robert needed to learn measurement, we measured everything—the living room, rainfall, the amount of milk he put on his morning cereal, even the weight of the cat, which wasn't easy," she says. "When it came to fractions, we baked our hearts out, ate pizza far too often, and we have a couple of wobbly tables Robert helped my husband build during that period. When he studied simple machines we rigged up a sheet on a pulley system to surround his bed; he was fascinated with it and played with it endlessly. When he began learning about other cultures and their traditions, we created some thoughtful traditions for our own family. Honestly," says Trish,

"I'd be astonished if he ever forgot any of these things."

Experience is greatly enhanced with the addition of time to experiment. Leave learning materials out and about, even after "the lesson" appears over. Not only will this help set the learning in stone through practice, it gives your child, if interested, a chance to figure out any why's or how's or where's he's still wondering about. She'll have a chance to ask and satisfy the curiosity that drives "what if I do this, instead," that leads to ever-deeper understanding.

Thomas Alva Edison made umpteen false starts before he lit up the world. He learned something during each experience that kept him experimenting until he got it right. Help your child establish these habits, let her use it so she doesn't lose it, and she just may light up the world in her own way someday.

CHAPTER 6

TRANSFORMING YOUR HOME INTO A LEARNING GYM

You don't create an NBA star without giving him some balls and baskets and giving him a place to use them in context. When it comes to coaching an athlete, it's obvious that an environment that provides lots of opportunity to exercise skills and practice, practice, practice are vital to success. Why not apply the same thinking as a learning coach? You can do the same for your young learner by transforming your home into a learning gym.

PURPOSE

A person intent on exercising, working out, and strengthening muscles goes to a specific place built for that purpose—a gym. The place is filled with the equipment and resources necessary to help her incrementally achieve her goal. The gym is filled with football, tennis, basketball, polo, baseball, and soccer players alike. They're not there to engage in their particular sport; rather they go about their routines utilizing the same equipment to build the muscles and strength they all need as a foundation in order to participate in their various specialized sports.

Similarly, your learning gym isn't intended to be a "math field" or "science court." Instead, it's a space filled with the equipment and resources necessary for activity that builds and strengthens mental power. It's a place where your child can turn to exercise the brain as a foundation, *before* moving out again to that math field and science court. This type of foundational exercise is often missing in class-rooms. "As far back as 1967," writes Kathryn S. Carr in an ERIC Clearinghouse on Elementary and Early Childhood Education paper called "How Can We Teach Critical Thinking?" researchers "decried the lack of emphasis on thinking in the schools. They noted that 'memorization, drill, homework, the three R's, and the quiet class-room' were rewarded, while '. . . inquiry, reflection, and the consideration of alternatives were frowned upon.'"

Inquiry, reflection, and consideration of alternatives —this is the stuff that builds brain power and promotes critical thinking. There are many similar definitions of critical thinking out there, but here's a simple one from Richard Paul, author of *Critical Thinking: How to Prepare Students for a Rapidly Changing World*: "Critical thinking is thinking about your thinking while you're thinking in order to make your thinking better."

Using your family's learning gym will help your child think for himself. As he grows and needs to make life-affecting decisions, today's exercise will help him do so reliably and responsibly. Pumping up the gray matter will help him solve problems and ask necessary questions. If necessary, it will help him to question and challenge the status quo, authorities, dogma, doctrine, and traditional beliefs in order to discover new information, or create new connections for existing information, for his own benefit or the benefit of his community.

CREATING A SPECIAL PLACE

What does a learning gym look like? How big is it? Where is it? The answers to these questions depend on your personal circumstances, the space available in your home, the traffic patterns of your space, and your child's preference to be amidst family hub-bub or in a quieter location.

Provide as much space for the learning gym as you can without making your child feel as if she's being banished into a chilly back room or the basement. (While I've had plenty of space for a bedroom-turned-office, I can't bear the idea of sitting in such a relatively small, isolated section of the house and choose instead to have the most highly-used aspect of my office—my computer desk—smack dab in the middle of the living space.) Your learning gym area can simply be a little-used corner—or one cleared out for the purpose. At a minimum it should include a comfortable chair (some children like bean bag chairs or floor cushions), a lap desk or other surface on which to write or lay reading materials, and good lighting. If space allows, include a chair and desk for writing and shelving. As always, get your child's input as to where she thinks she would like to spend the time and what personal effects she might like to place in her space.

Help your child make a sign, or have her make her own, designating "Megan's Learning Gym" or "Kelly's Critical Thinking Corner;" something that helps her recognize this as not just a special place, but a special place for her. Fill the wall space with significant sayings of her choosing, or with standard motivational quotes, such as "When the going gets tough, the tough get going" or "No strain, no bigger brain."

Remember that the concept of stretching one's mind for its own sake may feel quite foreign to your child. It will take some time to adjust to taking seriously anything that lacks necessity for a grade, test, or other assessment with regard to learning. On the positive side, this can help your child better enjoy the learning gym activities and eventually place them, rightfully so, into her everyday life.

CREATING ROUTINE

Any successful exerciser will tell you that it's slow-and-steady that wins the race. It's better to establish a routine of a minimal amount of time spent in the learning gym daily (or three times a week, or whatever fits best into your family's timetable) than it is to spend hours there on a haphazard schedule.

Upon returning home from school it's quite possible that your child is *physically* tired but, in many cases, not *mentally* tired, since much typical schoolwork doesn't strain the brain. This will likely be the best time for his workout—after a healthy snack and drink help him improve focus. Many children find that, as with athletes, the learning gym can serve as a "warm up," as it stretches the muscle necessary to help make tackling homework quicker and easier.

If your child is a real night owl, and/or you or your spouse would like to be integrally involved in learning gym activities, establish a good evening time to be in the learning gym. Many families find they easily make additional time when they don't turn on the television set at night.

Keep the workout short, at least at the beginning, until your child gets used to the idea; ten minutes for younger children, fifteen to twenty for older ones. Your child will soon discover that such a short period of time doesn't allow him to get very involved in anything and it's wonderful if he decides for himself that he wants to spend more time on his exercises. Whether it's ten minutes or an hour, provide a timer so he knows when the specific amount of time is up and moves on to other activities. If you or another adult cannot be present, it may be necessary to leave an "assignment" for him before you go out each morning. Once he establishes the routine and gets involved in his workouts, however, he'll likely need less prompting.

Have an "administrative" meeting for a few minutes with your child every weekend or once a month. Encourage him to share and talk about what he's been accomplishing. Find out what he really likes—or dislikes—and what he might like to do more often. In the beginning, assess his happiness and comfort with the location of his learning gym and make adjustments, if necessary. Keeping your knowledge of what motivates and interests him, as well as his intellectual strengths and dispositions, in mind you can offer guidance on maximizing the time he's spending in the gym.

COACH'S MOTIVATIONAL MINUTE: One day, much sooner than you can imagine, your child will have asked you to help with school work for the very last time. Embrace this moment today and enter her world, if only for a few moments. She has much to teach you; you have much to learn. Dinner, bills, and other obligations will wait; your opportunity to inspire and encourage will not.

LEARNING GYM RESOURCES

Your child is "working out" to stretch and strengthen that muscle we call the mind. Any resource that gets her thinking *about* her thinking *while* she's thinking so she learns to *think better* is a good one. You'll find lots of good starting materials in the sample resources box, and the more you work with these the easier it will become to recognize more when you see them. As with any other specialty there is jargon, or buzz words, to help indicate a resource's purpose. Here are a few to watch for as you consider purchasing resources: critical thinking; critical questioning; deductive, inductive, and logical reasoning; logical thinking; analytical thinking; problem-solving; mental organizational skills; higher order thinking skills; theorizing; perceptual skills, and critical analysis.

Purchase a few resources that help your child with test-taking skills, too. While test scores will always be important to teachers, administrators, future college admissions officers, and bosses, the skills necessary to take the tests, for the most part, aren't taught. Practicing taking a test won't necessarily make your child smarter, but it will help him feel more comfortable when presented with one. Combined with a growing ability to think better, this will eventually translate into greater school success.

Additionally, in discussions with coaches about choosing learning gym equipment, they mention two criteria almost universally. Experienced learning coaches recommend that first and foremost the learning resources on which you spend good money should be:

Ability-appropriate—Many specifically educational resources provide recommendations for use based on age. At times this provides a basis for making a good guesstimate as to suitability for your child.

It is, however, a very general basis. Rare is the child who is either excellent or terrible in every school subject. More often a child excels in some areas, is average in others, or has difficulty in still others. Using the age criteria alone you could wind up supplying materials that are either boringly non-challenging, or frustratingly out of whack with skill level which can give your child a sense of failure. As a learning coach, call upon your knowledge of your child's ability to help you decide on a product's appropriateness for her by ability as well as age.

Reachable—I remember so clearly when my children were small and I thought that leaving "the messy things" within their easy grasp would, quite logically, produce, well, messes. While my logic was infallible, I discovered that keeping fun, interesting, messy things out of my children's reach created far too many days that included conversations like this.

"Mom, I want to paint a picture of the cat in that story. I need the paints."

"Oh, honey, I'm in the middle of making dinner. Why don't you go play with your brother?"

"I don't want to play with him. I want to paint a picture of that cat when he got his paw stuck in the mouse hole. That was funny."

"Not now, darlin'. Later—we'll have to do it later, after dinner is cleaned up."

You know what happened? Far too often, the moment was never re-seized. Far too often, "later" never came. Quite naturally the would-be artist moved on to other activity, and that painting of a cat with his paw stuck in the mouse hole doesn't exist.

Is it easy for me to encourage you to let your child mess up your house? You bet it is! It's easy because I know that if you choose to clean up those messes today, one day in the not-very-distant-future, when the house is quiet and empty, you'll make a warm cup of tea, look at that painting of a cat with his paw stuck in the mouse hole, and smile.

SAMPLE MATERIALS FOR YOUR LEARNING GYM

Games

SET—A card game that challenges visual perception and thinking skills. Control the level of difficulty by choosing which cards to include, so all ages can play. Selected by Mensa and *Omni* as top mind game for 1991. Game objective: Identify a "set" of three cards from twelve cards laid on the table. Eighty-one cards have four variations: shape, color, number, and shading. Adjust challenge by limiting play to three attributes or starting with more cards on table. No reading required.

TIC TAC TWICE—Challenges thinking and reasoning skills. Simple rules for a game that results in some pretty impressive math skills where strategy, not luck, counts. Two players, ages 7 and up.

TRIOLOGY GAME—This winner of Games 100 Award is from the makers of *Set*. Combines the visual challenge of *Set*, the action of *War*, and the fun of *Rummy*. Two or more players, ages 8 and up.

CHESS

MANCALA

TANGRAMS

GEO-BOARD

LABYRINTH

BRAINTEASERS BY SQUARE ROOT GAMES

Puzzle and Brainteaser Sources

AREYOUGAME.COM

BITSANDPIECES.COM

BRAINPUZZLES.COM

BRAINGLE.COM (FREE/ONLINE)

EDUPLACE.COM/MATH/BRAIN

    (FREE/ONLINE/ESPECIALLY FOR KIDS)

Books and Workbooks

PRIVATE EYE: LOOKING AND THINKING BY ANALOGY—
Designed to develop higher order thinking skills and creativity
across the curriculum, this is a program about looking closely
at the world, theorizing, thinking by analogy, and changing
scale. Hands-on and investigative, child uses everyday materials, a jeweler's loupe, and questions to develop an
"interdisciplinary mind" through improved communication,
problem solving, and concentration skills. Grades K-12.

THINKING SKILLS PRACTICE BOOKS—Workbooks that
develop thinking skills such as qualification, comparing, con-
trasting, predicting, summarizing, concluding, and causation. Six
books, grades K–6.

BRAIN TEASERS AND SQUEEZERS by Mary Rosenberg

CRIME SCENE DETECTIVE: USING SCIENCE AND CRITICAL THINKING TO SOLVE CRIMES by Karen Schulz. Child develops critical thinking skills as she figures out who started the fire in the school library. Includes background information on forensics and exploration of careers in forensic science and law enforcement. Student examines evidence at the scene, interviews suspects, and uses thinking skills to connect clues and eliminate suspects. Also includes instructions to write your own crime scene simulation.

DESIGN STUDIO: INTEGRATING ART AND THINKING by Diane Draze and Annelise Palouda. A course in thinking that also teaches design principles: unity, repetition, color, balance, proportion, variety, movement, emphasis, economy, and space. Unique projects allow opportunity to hone thinking and artistic skills.

DETECTIVE CLUB. Solve six mysteries by decoding messages, sorting information, and thinking logically. Grades 2-4.

FAMOUS PEOPLE PUZZLES: EXERCISES IN INFERENCE AND RESEARCH by Carolyn Powell. The famous people are: Louis Armstrong, Julius Caesar, Jacques Cousteau, Marie Curie, Arthur Conan Doyle, Thomas Edison, Albert Einstein, Benjamin Franklin, Mahatma Gandhi, Nathaniel Hawthorne, Nelson Mandela, Edson Arantes do Nascinento (Pelé), Georgia O'Keeffe, Sacagawea, William Shakespeare, and Harriet

Tubman. Each of the 16 units contains general information for the instructor, personal momentos to be duplicated and given to your student, a reproducible page for research notes, and a reference log form. Using scraps of imagined papers left by these famous people, your child exercises deductive reasoning skills while fleshing out clues with research to find out who "wrote" the fragments. For grades 5-8.

LOLLIPOP LOGIC: CRITICAL THINKING ACTIVITIES by Bonnie and Robby Risby. Seven different thinking skills in 64 pages: relationships, analogies, sequences, deduction, inference, pattern decoding, and critical analysis. This book uses pictures rather than words for student response, so is suitable for non-readers. For grades K-2.

ONE-HOUR MYSTERIES by Mary Ann Carr. You have to be a detective with logic skills to solve this book's five crimes. Each mystery requires about one to three hours to solve and motivates students to learn reading and thinking skills. For grades 4-8.

LOGIC SAFARI SERIES. Deductive logic puzzles include the problem, the grid, and an eye-catching illustration. Book 1, grades 2-3; Book 2, grades 3-4; Book 3, grades 5-6.

QUOTATION QUIZZLERS: PUZZLING YOUR WAY THROUGH FAMOUS QUOTATIONS by Philip A. Steinbacher. Your child deciphers fifty quotations with critical and flexible thinking, word analysis, and ability to see the small pieces and their parts in the whole solution. Grades 5-8.

WORKING WITH ANALOGIES: MAKING CONNECTIONS BOOK 1 by Jim McAlpine, Betty Weincek, Sue Jeweler, and Marion Finkbinder. Analogies help children think about the relationships betweens words, pictures, and symbols, and this understanding transfers to reading comprehension and critical thinking. The book is divided into five sections: Part-to-Whole/Whole-to-Part; Synonyms and Antonyms; Purpose, Use, or Function; Cause and Effect; and Degree. Uses both visual/symbolic and verbal analogies, contains some open-ended exercises, and helps child learn how to create analogies. For grades 2-3.

YOU BE THE JUDGE: LESSONS TO BUILD EVALUATIVE THINKING SKILLS by Barbara Juskow. Lessons and reproducible worksheets introduce students to three types of decision making: criteria evaluations, value judgments, and judicial decisions. Each section contains several lessons that introduce an evaluative skill to be practiced. Participants weigh, consider, debate, and cast judgment after learning how to decide on criteria, how to use criteria to judge the best ideas, how values affect decisions, and more. For grades 5-8.

Test Preparation

SPECTRUM TEST PREP WORKBOOKS. Practice for skills and proficiency tests. Includes test-taking strategies and techniques, test questions in reading, language arts, writing, math, social studies, and science. Guidelines and advice for parents; study tips for students. Separate workbooks for grades 2-8 include answer key.

Miscellaneous

- CROSSWORD PUZZLES
- PALINDROMES
- CRYPTOGRAMS
- CRYPTIC CROSSWORDS
- ANAGRAMS
- WRITING JOURNAL
- VARIETY OF PAPER, PENS, AND ART SUPPLIES
- HTTP://WWW.EDHELPER.COM/LOGIC_PUZZLES.HTM
  Customizable, critical thinking logic puzzles online
- *QUICK PICK ACTIVITIES FOR CRITICAL THINKING.* 120 activity cards in a box to help kids build ability to recall, comprehend, analyze, synthesize, evaluate, and extend responses. Cards are color-coded for easy filing and icons identify activity type; space for notes on back. Includes user's guide and assessment checklist. Level 1 (ages 5-7); Level 2 (ages 7-9); Level 3 (ages 9-11)
- HTTP://PUZZLES.CLEVERSOUL.COM/MG_MENSA.HTML
  Selection of Mensa for Kids puzzle books
- CRITICALTHINKING.COM—Materials for PreK-Adult

LOVING SUPPORT AND ENCOURAGEMENT

Finally, remember to continue offering loving support and encouragement as your child works hard to stretch and build mental power. She's used to receiving grades and stars as rewards; as learning coach you can replace these with continual motivation, praise, and appreciation of accomplishment. Keep the activities cooperative and not competitive, especially if there are two or more siblings working out together. No one ever likes to be considered less intelligent than another, and this is especially true between brothers and sisters.

Dr. Gerald Jampolsky, founder of the Center for Attitudinal Healing, recommends that we eliminate a few words from our conversation with children to help create a more positive environment during their formative years. The list is applicable to our work as learning coaches in our learning gyms, too.

WORDS TO ELIMINATE

Impossible	Difficult	Terrible
Can't	Must	Demand
Try	Should	But
Limitation	Doubt	Insist
If Only	Awful	Ought To
However	Horrible	Always

As a learning coach you are in a unique position not only to help build your child's brain power, but to do it in an environment that honors his individual needs, strengths, and interests in love. Transform your home into a learning gym, and watch your child blossom.

CHAPTER 7

BRINGING OUT THE BEST IN YOUR CHILD: BASIC COACHING TECHNIQUES

O K, coach, you're training yourself with new habits, you're continuing your book learning, you're observing your child, you know the habits of successful learners, and your learning gym is coming together. It's time for your game plan!

In the next three chapters we will explore a variety of coaching techniques for day-to-day life. While they're divided into three categories for organization's sake, the lines between the categories are fluid and you should use whatever works with your child for the circumstances at hand. We'll also revisit some of the ideas introduced in previous chapters, both to expand upon them and keep them handy for future reference. The resultant benefits of the techniques are also noted for cross-referencing purposes. This way, if you see your child could use a little help with initiative, for example, you can easily spot a technique, such as challenging your child to greater heights, that accomplishes this goal.

As you read the next three chapters, think about how you might implement each technique with your child, or each of your unique children, if you have more than one. Keep in mind: *Curiosity creates interest, interest increases attention to the task at hand, and attention gives rise to learning.* Free up your imagination to invent new, different, and more fun ways to accomplish what may have become routine drudgery. There are no right and wrong ways to use these techniques. Despite your deepest fears, you won't do something so "wrong" that you ruin your child forever. You are so intimately and integrally involved that you will know immediately that something isn't going right or isn't working. If, by chance, that happens, you change course immediately. Easy, yes? Instead of fretting, spend more time thinking that you could do something so "right" as to make your child happier, more content, and more successful than your family ever imagined was possible.

COACHING TECHNIQUE: ANSWER QUESTIONS

BENEFITS: Builds confidence, promotes enthusiasm and interest, gives rise to a sense of wonder

What does this do? What happens if you turn it the other way? How does that work? What are you going to do with it? Why?

(Unless we're in the worst of moods), small children can be extremely endearing with their many wide-eyed questions that we answer daily. Maybe it's because through those questions we glimpse their unspoiled, still-as-yet-uncensored sense of wonder. Maybe it's because we're provided with a hint of the innate desire to understand and participate in the world, the same one with which we were born but tend to lose touch with over time. Whatever the reason, it's wonderful, it's natural, and as adults we welcome and accept it as such.

As children grow, though, at some point teachers and parents alike begin to respond quite illogically. Instead of simply answering questions, we begin shooting questions right back. "Well, Johnny, how do *you* think you spell it?" "What country do *you* think it's near?" "How do *you* think it works?" We may as well save everyone time and ask the child directly, "How frustrated can I get you?"

We wouldn't dream of doing this to our spouses, co-workers, or mailmen. Yet as if by an unspoken universal agreement this becomes routine handling of school-aged children's questions. Learning coaches need to look at it another way. If he's asking for information, it means he's curious about it at the moment. If the goal is for an inquiring child to learn, doesn't it makes more sense to provide that information while interest is at its height so the child can immediately use it and continue the activity in which he is engaged?

Maxine knew that responding to her two children's questions with questions was common practice in her family's home, "because that's the way it was when both my husband and I grew up," she says. "I think it started when they were about eight or nine-years-old, when they were getting old enough to look things up on their own. At first I thought of it as good practice for them, but once I started observing I could see it was a source of frustration, and that the negative consequence outweighed any positive benefit."

As a leaning coach, Maxine figures that about 50 percent of the time she can answer a question without breaking stride in whatever she happens to be doing at the moment. The other 50 percent of the time is a bit more demanding.

"I do my best to answer immediately," says Maxine, "but that's not always possible, so the boys are aware of my own little rule; nothing waits more than twenty-four hours. If I don't address it in a timely manner, they have the right to bug me until I do. They love that, and it's more than enough impetus to keep me from delaying."

On such occasions, Maxine turns car trips, errands, grocery store line waits, waiting room time, breakfast, dinner, and bedtimes into discussion time. "It works for us," says the satisfied mom. "There is *one* exception to the rule, and that's if I don't know the answer which, as the boys get older, happens more frequently. I keep a list of such questions on the refrigerator, and on Saturday mornings we do whatever we have to do to find the answers together. Thank goodness, most often it's the Internet in the comfort of home, but sometimes we go to the library for books or videotapes, make phone calls to people we think might know, or might know someone who knows, or write letters to individuals, businesses, or agencies— wherever we think there may be an answer.

"We've done this long enough that they're growing very confident in being able to find out **whatever** they want to know, and they often make recommendations on where to look for answers. Just the other day Matt, the older, confessed that he tries hard to come up with dif- ficult questions, partly as a challenge to me. And you know," Maxine adds, "I'm learning just as much as they are."

COACHING TECHNIQUE:
GIVE IMMEDIATE FEEDBACK

BENEFITS: Promotes focus, adds context to learning, builds confidence, builds understanding of the thinking process, gives rise to a sense of wonder

Remember Professor C's theory of flow, which he defines as "exceptional moments that create the sense of effortless action people feel in moments that stand out as the best in their lives"? Even though the professor is focused on what makes life worth living, and I on the study of fun, effective learning, we both arrived in a remarkably similar place. Here's another of Professor C's points about the exceptional life moments called flow: "When goals are clear, feedback relevant, and challenges and skills are in balance, attention becomes ordered and fully invested. Because of the total demand on psychic energy, a person in flow is completely focused."

Much of the academic feedback a child receives in school is, by virtue of the system, delayed. When twenty, twenty-five , or thirty children in a class turn in a project, experiment, drawing, story, book report, or test result all at the same time (and as children get older the odds increase that their teachers have more than one class doing the same thing at the same time), immediate feedback is impossible.

"In second grade, Brian would turn in homework or take a test on Monday and get feedback by Wednesday or so," explains April, whose family of three lives not far from Brian's school. "Then as he passed through third and fourth grades the time lag increased until now, in fifth grade, he's lucky if that feedback comes within a week. As that week passes by they start studying something totally different, so when they finally review the test nothing on it is 'front and center' in the kids' minds. The icing on the cake," April continues, "is that the test sheets often only have the multiple choice or true or false answers. A week later the kids are told 'the answer to 1 was 'b,' the answer to 2 was false. A kid would have to be *really* interested to go through the trouble to check where he went wrong. And most aren't," April concludes.

Using immediate feedback as a coaching technique keeps learning in its immediate context. After all, whether it was something he was doing or just thinking about, this something spurred a comment or question, and immediate feedback keeps the new knowledge in context, advancing the learning experience. It also contributes to focus, supports CIAL to improve your child's learning experience and, according to Professor C, it will also raise your child's happiness quotient at the same time.

We can think about the fact that immediate feedback, just like the previous technique, is something adults receive and provide to each other all the time. Show up late for the big meeting; receive relevant, immediate feedback. Lose your queen in a chess game, relevant, immediate feedback. Again we can ask: If the goal is for a child to learn, and we have the opportunity to provide information in the form of an immediate lesson, isn't it wise for a parent to provide it?

When you blend learning into your daily routine, you increase opportunities to provide immediate feedback. In this way you don't interrupt your child's thought processes or interfere with the goal of the moment. Learning remains in the context of the task at hand.

COACHING TECHNIQUE: FACILITATE THE ACT OF LEARNING

BENEFITS: Builds confidence, promotes enthusiasm and interest, kindles curiosity, gives rise to a sense of wonder, increases initiative, builds understanding of the thinking process

This technique sounds simple, but that's deceiving. We have such a propensity toward teaching a child that it's hard to get out of the way and let the natural learning process unfold. Yet when you as learning coach make a conscious effort not to block progress, the ways in which you can facilitate instead become obvious.

Lillian, learning coach to Ethan, now grown and in college, explained this beautifully in a piece she wrote in response to a question for my book *The Homeschooling Book of Answers: The 88 Most Important Questions Answered by Homeschooling's Most Respected Voices* . "Life," Lillian begins, "offers so many things that are fun to learn, interesting to learn, good to learn, or necessary to learn, but formal lessons are not generally helpful for the learning process—

there's something clumsily unnatural about them.

"A young child wants to learn about the world, about people, animals, places, the seasons, weather, the night sky, the sun and moon, processes like plant's growth—all things that come about naturally in the course of living, questioning, and observing. If you pay sensitive attention, it will be obvious when your child is ready to learn something.

"Any learning," Lillian continues, "can be approached in just the same way as helping a child get a kite off the ground; you can be a partner in learning rather than a teacher. Children will also learn an amazing amount on their own, and you'll recognize this more and more throughout the years. If you provide trips into the wider world—a good play environment, good conversation, construction toys, books, tools, craft supplies, dolls, and models—their growth and learning will flourish.

"Parents' worries behind the issue of 'lessons' are usually around the question of discipline, or whatever might need to be mastered for college entrance exams, and academic success toward a career. This is where you might want to seriously reexamine the nature of learning. A child can labor for years over those things from an early age, or he can wait until much later, and get through them pretty quickly. If he's had a healthy childhood, with plenty of time for growth and exploration, his enthusiasm and imagination will be ready for meeting the challenge later. Parents often worry about how they can teach something they don't know about or don't remember; but parents tend to underestimate the ability of kids to learn on their own, or better yet, alongside their parents."

When next you're tempted to teach your child, remember the definition of "to facilitate"—to free from difficulties or obstacles; make easier; aid; assist. Use the analogy of your child needing to take a hike. You want to help him complete it. With the emphasis on completion, as it is with teaching, you might decide to carry him the entire way, making him a passive recipient of the hike. The goal—completion—is accomplished. Now think of your child accomplishing that goal, not because you carried him, but because you accompanied him, pointing out the flora and fauna, answering his questions, moving a fallen log blocking his path, carrying a first aid kit in case it's needed. In this way, the experience, and the learning belong to him as an active participant. He experiences a sense of accomplishment and he grows more confident that he can do it again, or hike farther in rougher terrain. You helped by aiding and removing obstacles, but he, the hiker, is the star. You facilitate your child's learning by hiking the learning path with him.

COACH'S MOTIVATIONAL MINUTE: There's a reason the saying, "If Momma ain't happy, ain't nobody happy" has stuck around as long as it has. Take time to replenish your own energy so you stay healthy and strong for coaching. Enlist the help of your spouse whenever possible—and make sure you allow yourselves time alone as a couple, too. Decide what's really important in your life—then cut out the rest. There will be plenty of time for other things when your child reaches the goal of independence. Now is when she needs your time as learning coach.

COACHING TECHNIQUE:
SHARE YOUR OWN EXPERIENCE

BENEFITS: Adds context to learning, improves problem solving skills, builds understanding of the thinking process

When Stacie returned home after work in the emergency room as a registered nurse, not only was she tired, she didn't think her son, John, age eight nor her daughter, Dianna, age eleven, were interested in what she did. She began sharing her daily experiences during dinner and bedtime, anyway, and received a pleasant surprise.

"I began with just a couple of minutes of what I thought they'd find most interesting," Stacie explains. "At first they listened but didn't really comment. After about a week of this, though, they began asking questions; about procedures, and about the patients and my co-workers. This was the beginning of something wonderful," she says.

Once Stacie hooked the children's interest, "mostly through stories of blood and guts," she admits, her stories began to include more explanations of how and why she used math every day. She relayed problems as mysteries, and soon the children were offering their own guesses as to how they were solved, as well as recommendations for "next time." She outlined standard operating procedure for different traumas, and explained the thinking process and logic behind each.

"No one was more surprised than me to find out that John had been relaying what he was learning to his friends in his Cub Scout pack, and they all wanted to visit!" says a pleased Stacie. "There was a noticeable increase in interest when we used math around the house, too, and who knows where that might lead. Oh," Stacie adds,

"I'm also working on a book for kids incorporating some of our discussions. It would be wonderful if other children got hooked, too, wouldn't it?"

As you share your own experiences with your child, don't forget to tell her about the mistakes you or others made. Tell her what the consequences were, if you felt embarrassed, and how you corrected the problem. Defend your position, if appropriate. This, too, provides many valuable lessons, such as the fact that things don't always go right, even for the grown-ups who are supposed to know *everything*. It reveals problem-solving techniques, and furnishes a storehouse of information your child may not be able to use today, but will be able to draw upon in the future when needed. On top of all of this, it proves to your child the human condition of imperfection.

COACHING TECHNIQUE: FOCUS ON IMPROVEMENT, NOT HONOR SOCIETY MEMBERSHIP

BENEFITS: Builds confidence, promotes enthusiasm and interest, increases self-responsibility

It happens to the best of parents. Perhaps it happens to the best of parents most of all. We give our child's academic performance power to be the defining factor of our parenting skills. If a child is doing well in school, aren't we wonderful parents! If a child isn't doing so well, aren't we terrible!

You can drive yourself crazy with this all too false assessment. Worse, you can drive your child absolutely nuts by transferring to her, however indirectly, all of your own insecurities and self-doubt. A most rewarding aspect of being a learning coach, for both you and your child, is that you needn't worry about grades, comparisons to peers, or the National Honor Society. Instead, you can focus on fun, significance to life, and personal improvement.

Grasping the multiplication tables when he's months behind his classmates isn't a direct route into that Honor Society. It is, however, a direct path to self-confidence, increased self-responsibility, and competence in the adult world we (and he) know he will soon enter. Lucinda, a stay-at-home mom of three, learned the hard way the importance of focusing on personal improvement with her eldest child, Marquetta.

"No one in either of our families has gone to college, and we have high hopes to change that with all our children," Lucinda begins. "It started for Marquetta in kindergarten—members of two large, extended families constantly checking on what she was learning, how she was doing. Relatives would come over and have her cram when standardized tests came around, telling her she had to do well and be at the top of her class. When she was in third grade," Lucinda continues, "she got sick and missed a week of school. She didn't want to go back. Every other day she had a stomachache or a headache, she didn't do homework, her grades dropped, and she was depressed all the time."

Lucinda happened to catch brief coverage of the growing stress on schoolchildren on a news program one evening and it described Marquetta's condition perfectly. "I spoke with all our family members and told them 'enough,' that we were pressing her too hard," says Lucinda. "We were so worried about her grades we forgot to worry about *her*."

The transition to concentrating on personal achievement didn't come easily to the family, but they persevered. Instead of asking Marquetta about tests, they inquired as to what she was studying, and what was most interesting about it. Instead of asking how many other children got a better grade than she did, they reinforced their belief in her intelligence, perseverance, and ability. Instead of watching her grades go down, they noticed that, slowly, they were rising again.

Determined to make the situation even better, and spurred in part by noticing a similar decline in Marquetta's siblings' spirits, Lucinda also turned learning into a household affair instead of relying solely on the school. "I made up games that let the kids use what they were learning in school," she explains. "Once I saw they were enjoying this, I turned them into what I think they call 'friendly competition.' But it was competition against *themselves*, like completing seven arithmetic calculations in a minute, breaking his or her previous record of six, or in the evening finding on the globe all ten countries on the list I gave them instead of just half of them. Soon I didn't need to constantly tell them they were doing better; they could see it for themselves! Marquetta is smiling again." Lucinda concludes, "Oh, how I missed that smile."

Separate your sense of self-worth from your child's academic standing. No one on earth is good at everything, and your child is good at many things. Celebrate her as an individual. Keep your eye on the big picture: a healthy, happy, responsible adult ready to make her way in the world independently. When she gets there, the Honor Society will be a part of her past, and her classmates will scatter to the four winds, revealing them as insignificant, inaccurate yardsticks. Having grown up aware of the benefits of personal improvement, she'll carry with her the best and only yardstick she'll ever need.

CHAPTER 8

COACHING TECHNIQUES TO INSPIRE JOY AND INDEPENDENCE

Every once in a while we're treated to a news story about a young hero. A little boy calls On-Star when his mother suddenly becomes ill in the car. A four-year-old girl calls 911 and saves Grandpa's life when he has an accident. A young Boy Scout rescues a man from drowning.

Such children seem almost an aberration when they rise to responsibility. Maybe it's because in general children are so rarely given the opportunity to show us their stuff. Of course we hope there's never such extremes in our lives during which our offspring might prove this degree of responsibility, but there is much space between "no responsibility" and life threatening emergencies.

Herbert Walberg and Susan Paik of the University of Illinois at Chicago noted in an article called "Home Environments for

Learning" (in the book *Psychology and Education Practice*, Walberg and Haertel, eds., McCutchan Publishing, 1997) that "through the formative years . . . until the end of high school, parents influence directly or indirectly 87 percent of the student's waking time that is spent outside school including children's neighborhood, peer-group, and other activities. This is by far the largest fraction of the student's life, and it strongly influences the productivity of the time spent in school."

The coaching techniques in this chapter will help you facilitate your child's learning because they're centered on emotional forces like motivation, morale, interest, and curiosity, many of the variables that affect learning. They are simple things you can do as learning coach to treat your child as the intelligent individual she is during these very influential years with her.

You may be surprised by how much your child is capable of. A little girl yearns to wear her mother's clothes and earrings, and a little boy can't stay away from Dad's garage tools. The desire to learn on the journey towards independence is innate. Capitalize on this desire and learning is truly a joyful experience. Help your child learn to resolve, on his own or with minimal help, most any basic domestic or life problem or task that confronts him, and independence is merely a series of life lessons away. A problem-solving tenacity will serve him well, not only in public school, but later in adult life as he is confronted with one seemingly irresolvable problem after another.

COACHING TECHNIQUE:
DELEGATE RESPONSIBILITY

BENEFITS: Builds confidence, increases self-responsibility, improves decision-making skills, promotes enthusiasm and wonder, increases initiative, builds concentration

A common complaint of working adults is, "The boss micro-manages everything I do. He never delegates decisions to me." Many children could utter the same complaint, feeling that the "bosses" of the house don't have any confidence in them. If constantly made to feel incompetent, children begin to believe it, then soon act out their beliefs. They carry the same feeling into the schoolhouse where it manifests itself over and over again. If it's not nipped in the bud, the no-confidence gremlin can become a monster of failure that haunts the ability to succeed. It is much better to give your child a chance to handle a task, make her own mistakes, learn the consequences of those mistakes, incrementally improve accomplishment skills, and receive both the negative stimuli of "messing up a bit" and the positive reinforcement of tackling a task and handling it reasonably well.

Learning coach Jessie decided to put the responsibility theory to the test in the grocery store with her eight-year-old son, Gary. "His tasks were to watch the clock to make sure we weren't gone from home too long," Jessie explains. "He also had to look at the coupons and find the correct items as we shopped. It was great! He did well with the tasks, but the neatest thing is that he *really* enjoyed himself—and wants to do it again."

Jessica began with simple tasks that Gary could learn and handle with initial parental guidance. It's important not to come up with meaningless "child-like" tasks that have no functional applicability to home or the real world. Contrary to the trend of superficial self-esteem building, your child will know if he's being patronized.

Jessica followed through by making a list of common, simple, but important and meaningful household tasks that Gary could handle, tasks he knows Mom and Dad handle every day. If you choose to make a list, here are some of Jessica's ideas to get you started:

- Feed and groom the pets
- Organize the pantry shelves (at least as high as your child can reach)
- Water the plants
- Participate in emergency planning—fire escape routes, calling 911, draw up a house evacuation plan
- Bring in the mail
- Set the dinner table
- Add needed items to the grocery list
- Check the farm animals, count the funds in the family business cash register at the end of the day, or anything else specific to your family

Delegated tasks can be extended in duration (as the necessary attention span develops) and challenge level as your child masters the simpler ones, and as he grows in both stature and coordination. As her skills increase, so will her self-confidence. This provides her with an edge in the classroom, boosting her through difficult times, just as it will later in life when constantly told that something can't be done, or she faces a seemingly irresolvable problem. When your child develops self-confidence at home, he'll know he has the true grit to handle whatever he is called upon to do at school.

COACHING TECHNIQUE:
GREAT EXPECTATIONS
(EXPECT THE BEST BUT NOT MORE)

BENEFITS: Promotes enthusiasm and interest, builds confidence, increases initiative, promotes focus, builds concentration

In the last chapter we met Marquetta, who through her family's good intentions became a victim of what in today's lingo might be called "extreme expectations." They overwhelmed her, affected her physical, mental, and emotional health, and produced results contrary to those desired. Balance plays a crucial role while utilizing this particular technique. Expectations aren't great unless they're balanced, because only then are they tailored to fit your child perfectly. They provide enough of a challenge to keep her stretching toward greater heights of achievement, which improves what is already otherwise a wonderful thrill and sense of satisfaction, while the challenge also offers the opportunity to succeed.

Valerie and Jacob, who just moved into an isolated farmhouse, were rightfully concerned about what might happen in case of a fire. They put great expectations to the test with their eight year-old son, Erik. "If the smoke alarm goes off," Jacob asked the boy, "or if you found smoke or fire in the house, who do you think should do what, when, where, and why?"

Erik thought for a moment and responded, "I should get the dog and cat, then tell you and Mom, and then dial 911 before trying to put out the fire." While Valerie and Jacob were a tad hurt that the well-being of the dog and cat took precedence over Mom and Dad, they were impressed with Erik's practical suggestions. They kicked up the expectations a notch. "We put him in charge of writing up fire escape procedures with the understanding that we'd discuss and possibly improve upon them as a family team," Valerie says. Erik worked hard for several days, knowing this was important, understanding that his parents expected something that might save lives one day.

COACH'S MOTIVATION MINUTE: Treat yourself to great expectations, too. Transforming your family's habits and lifestyle takes time. If you put too much pressure on yourself to accomplish too much too quickly, you won't do anything with a smile on your face, and that will defeat the purpose of everything you're doing. Smile and be joyful, too!

"His plan wouldn't have won the Nobel Prize for literature," says Jacob, "but we could tell he was proud to live up to our expectations. We praised what was good, explained how some things could be improved, and made suggestions to flesh out the plan, which he followed through with. When he was done Valerie typed it up and Erik posted copies around the house and in the barn. When an impressed visitor remarked about the plan, Erik told him, 'I did it sort of all by myself.'"

COACHING TECHNIQUE:
GIVE THE GIFT OF LIFE SKILLS

BENEFITS: Kindles curiosity, builds confidence, promotes enthusiasm and interest, increases self- responsibility, improves problem-solving skills, increases initiative, builds understanding of the thinking process, adds context to learning

Umberto, eighty-nine-years-old, grew up in El Paso, and his Italian mother did it all for everyone, not just in the kitchen but the entire house. Umberto never had to lift a finger, except to practice the piano that his immigrant parents believed would give him a leg up in the system. Eventually Umberto married a traditional woman who also did it all, "just like Mama," he said. "My wife died fifty-nine years later and I was alone for the first time. I didn't know how to turn on the kitchen range, shop for food, and I couldn't run the washer and dryer." Lacking basic self-care skills, it wasn't long before Umberto had to move out of his home into an assisted living residence. When he passed away, a fellow resident helping to clear out Umberto's belongings said, "Poor guy, he didn't even know how to put a button on a good shirt, and there it hung in a closet for ten years because he was too proud to ask anyone to sew it on for him."

For the first time in the country's demographic history, the number of "children" in their twenties and thirties returning home after being away for a while is sharply rising. While the states of the economy and the job market certainly are factors, some believe the advent of the "boomerang generation" is also attributable to a lack of life skills needed for independent living.

Umberto's saga and the growing trend of returning children make it clear we do children a grave disservice if we don't pass on basic life skills that are vital to survival. The earlier you start the better, because you can capitalize on the younger child's desire to help and be included in "adult stuff." Incorporate your child into the simple but important day-to-day requirements of running a household. Allow the nature of your domestic and business life to dictate what's important and valuable to know.

As you review the upcoming areas of life skills, don't ascribe areas based on gender. A man who can cook, clean the house, sew, and do the laundry is pretty attractive when later in life he enters the marriage market. Likewise, a gal who's not afraid to climb a ladder or get her hands dirty while changing the car's oil filter isn't going to marry for the wrong reasons.

Grocery Shopping, Nutrition, and Cooking

Hardly a day goes by that a news report doesn't warn Americans that we're eating too much saturated fat, sugar, and "white" food. We're not eating enough fruits and vegetables, and many diets don't contain enough calcium. Many of us, it appears, grew into adulthood without an understanding of basic nutrition.

Every family member will benefit when the learning coach picks up a book about nutrition at the library or bookstore and studies it. Share what you're learning as you read, because I guarantee you that your child will remember something you forget. Put your new-found knowledge to work together during what you should plan to be an extended trip to the grocery store. (If you want to make it shorter, you don't even have to buy groceries while there.)

"We only had an hour, so I didn't plan to shop when we did this exercise," says Roberta of her first learning excursion to the supermarket with Andrew, age seven and Jess, age ten. "It was the first time in my life I ever walked into a grocery store to learn instead of buy food, and it felt equally strange at first to the kids. But each boy took one of our two lists. One was of our questions about foods we knew we like and are good for us, but didn't know much about nutritional value, calories, sodium content of our favorite brand, and such. The other list," Roberta adds, "was of foods we didn't normally purchase, and we wanted to learn more about their nutritional value, as well as whether they were available fresh, frozen, canned, packaged, whatever, and how much they cost.

"After we got on a roll, Andrew and Jess had me running back and forth through the store as they hollered, 'Hey, guess what I found!' or 'Look at this, Mom, boy this is expensive!' An hour flew by in a flash and we had to go," says Roberta. "We hadn't completed our lists, though, and the boys asked if we could return, which we did."

COACH'S MOTIVATIONAL MINUTE: You don't have to stop at the grocery store. You can turn a rainy Saturday morning into a family learning experience with a trip to Lowe's, Home Depot, or your local hardware store. See all those pieces and gadgets you know nothing about? Ask a clerk to explain to you and your child what they're for. Pick up copies of the do-it-yourself literature for perusal at home. You might discover a home improvement project you can do together, or reviewing the material might spark some creative ideas in your family members.

After you go to the grocery store and actually shop, it's time to cook those nutritious foods, creating healthier, happier learners in your home. This skill will be worth its weight in gold to your independent child as prepared food typically costs a whopping fifty to one hundred percent more than fixing it yourself. And even the most devout pizza lover, I'm told, grows tired of devouring it six days a week.

READ IT AND EAT
(BOOKS ABOUT NUTRITION)

For Adults

• *The Family Nutrition Book: Everything You Need to Know about Feeding Your Children — from Birth through Adolescence* by William Sears

• *Quick Meals for Healthy Kids and Busy Parents: Wholesome Family Recipes in Thirty Minutes or Less from Three Leading Child Nutrition Experts* by Sandra K. Nissenberg, et. al.

• *How to Get Kids to Eat Great and Love It* by Dr. Christine Wood

For Children

• Ages 4-8: *The Edible Pyramid: Good Eating Every Day* by Loreen Leedy

• Ages 9-12: *The Race Against Junk Food: Adventures in Good Nutrition* by Anthony Buono, et. al.

• Ages 9-12; *Janice Van Cleave's Food and Nutrition for Every Kid: Easy Activities that Make Learning Science Fun* by Janice Van Cleave

Yes, initially it will take a little more time to include your protégée in the kitchen, but the rewards are worth it. As former editor of Suite101.com's Early Learning at Home page, Susan Franklin, wrote in an article titled "Early Learning in the Home—Kitchen Fun," "Shouldn't the kitchen be a place where our children feel comfortable to help out, ask questions, and learn about weighing and measuring, reading recipes, kitchen safety, and the basics of cooking and baking, not to mention to get their hands dirty and to clean up after themselves?"

Cooking, learning coach Yvette found out, helped dispel her nine year-old daughter, Megan's, fear of math and fractions, and showed the utility of numbers as they relate to measures and temperature settings. "Not only that," says Yvette, "there are so many little things that can be done to prepare non-fat, non-sugary yet tasty things for the family. Together we learned that Canola or olive oil is the best to use, and that after pre-cooking fries in the microwave we could then fry them with very little oil in the pan."

Yvette also saw to it that her daughter developed her own "secret recipes." All family members, but especially Megan's little brother, Todd, often say, "Megan, will you please make those yummy sweet potatoes?"

"She keeps experimenting and, of course, keeps learning because requests make her feel needed and appreciated," Yvette says, "especially after Thanksgiving, when the entire family was here. They, too, loved her recipe and she was thrilled with the attention and praise she received."

Healthy cooking leads to a healthy body and mind in optimum shape for learning. Include your kitchen in your coaching and not only will you impart a useful life skill, you'll help your child achieve a long and healthy life relatively free of heart disease, diabetes, and other debilitating illnesses linked to poor diet. Have your child bring home the school cafeteria menu, and help him recognize the no-no's on the menu. Spend a rainy Sunday afternoon preparing several nutritious "substitute" lunches so he'll know how to fix something when the menu selection for a particular day is simply not good eating for a successful learner.

Cleaning and House Care and Operation

In fifteen to twenty years, your child will likely make a purchase through which he will incur the single largest debt of his life. Will he know how to take care of it?

We all live in some sort of shelter, yet many of us—and almost all of our children—don't think twice about how things like plumbing, electricity and circuit breakers, hot and cold water, septic systems or sewers, insulation, and ventilation work—that is, until they don't work. You, as learning coach, can help your child think "outside the box" of how "everyone else does (or doesn't do) it." You can help him think globally, thus establishing the habit which will be carried to school, of considering the larger picture. One day learning coach Matt pointed out to his son, nine year-old Adam, that he used the toilet every day, and asked the boy how the system worked.

"You push the handle, water comes in, and cleans it out," Adam responded.

"Are we on a public sewer system or do we have a septic system?" Matt asked. The boy had no idea.

"We're on a septic system," Matt told Adam, "and we're having trouble with it. Come out and give me a hand to figure out what's wrong." Father and son spent the rest of the afternoon digging and clearing clogs as Matt patiently explained how everything worked. When the work was done, Adam asked what the family needed to do to make sure this didn't need to be done again. "It was the smell that prompted him to take a vested interest in making sure he didn't have to do that again anytime soon," says Matt, smiling. "It gave me a chance to talk with him about harsh detergents and soaps that kill the bacteria necessary to keep the system running smoothly, and why we use baking soda and vinegar for cleaning as often as possible. Adam learned a *lot* that afternoon."

From dusting to window washing, from septic tank function to landscaping, there's a lot to learn about maintaining one's investment in a home. Don't know about all these things? Then in true learning coach fashion, learn alongside your protégée. Become a role model of the principles of exploration and analysis, research and discovery. Encourage your child to ask questions. In "Creating True Collaborations," (find online by typing author and article name into search engine) Julia Harris and LaTida Lester explain, "Effective questions draw upon established knowledge and encourage exploration, developing skills that are applicable to a range of real-world situations. Parents can help their children reason through their challenges by asking questions such as: What have you tried? Would drawing a picture help? Can you make a chart? Is there a pattern? Have you done a similar problem? By asking these kinds of questions and participating with their children in the discovery process, parents are released from the need to have all the answers and instead become co-learners."

LEARNING AROUND THE HOUSE

- How does a circuit breaker box work?
- What does overloading a circuit mean, how does it happen, and why is it dangerous?
- What types of electrical appliances most often cause this?
- What is the major source of house fires?
- What is the best temperature for a hot water heater for cost savings and comfort?
- How do you turn down the thermostat on a hot water heater?
- What type of insulation is in your home?
- How should proper attic ventilation work?
- What things commonly found in most homes are bad for health?
- What are "green products" and products that help save the environment?
- Where do we shut off the main water supply in an emergency?
- How do we safely disconnect the main electrical supply in an emergency?
- What should be done in case of fire? When, where, and how?
- How does the garbage disposal work?
- How does the septic or sewer system work?

Personal Healthy, Hygiene, and Clothing Care

Can you imagine how many cold and flu epidemics could be avoided if children learned to consistently wash their hands and not put them in their mouths? Or how about children saying no to vast amounts of sugar and fast foods? Knowing how much water they should drink each day?

Impossible? Optimistic, perhaps, but not impossible. As parent you have a tremendous influence on your child's personal health and hygiene. As learning coach, you can see to it that good habits are established early and reinforced daily. You don't need a degree in Public Health, just a few good books from the library that give you guidance in what your child needs to know.

"I'll admit I used to dodge the issue of good health practices with my kids," says Sonya, learning coach to two daughters ages nine and twelve. "My husband and I were so guilty of failing to practice what we might preach, we didn't preach at all. A perfect example is that my husband smokes, so we never talked about it. When I finally screwed up my courage and did," she says, "I discovered they knew it was bad and that their Dad couldn't help himself. They understood—and love him, anyway, accepting the contradiction. I'd tell any other parent not to let your own bad habits stop you from sharing good ones with your kids, even if you're a poor messenger."

COACH'S MOTIVATIONAL MINUTE: Many American children are becoming couch potatoes and computer vegetables. This doesn't have to happen to your child. In a book by Billye Ann Cheatum and Allison A. Hammond called *Physical Activities for Improving Children's Learning and Behavior: A Guide to Sensory Motor Development*, they list 99 physical activities and games designed to help a disabled child enhance his physical and mental well being. And please don't accept some teacher's evaluation that your child is "clumsy." The book's authors show you how to overcome any such "diagnosis."

A FEW STARTING PLACES
FOR DISCUSSING HEALTHY LIVING

- Smoking and drinking
- A thorough shower or wash up every night (including use of nail brush on fingers and toes every few days)
- Family pets need to be washed before jumping into a human's bed
- Mosquitoes *may* carry West Nile virus
- Daily aerobic exercise

Children's clothing is big business, and a family can break the bank trying to keep up with new fads as dictated by a child's peers. Start now to teach life skills by caring for those clothes. Even very young children can help with the laundry, put theirs and others' clean laundry away, and operate the washer and dryer under your watchful eye. As your child gets older, an occasional lesson in ironing and sewing on buttons, torn pockets, and hems will not only save you a little time, but will increase your child's respect for the investment made on her behalf. We need these skills our entire lives. This is particularly true of little boys whose moms do it all, and who later encounter women who have no intention of taking care of them in that way. If nothing else, you'll certainly help him later in life when it comes to having a happy marriage.

Another topic about which learning coach's could feel uncomfortable is sex education. Yet with sexually transmitted disease (STD) and HIV-AIDS still alive and well in our culture, it's a must. Your child may know a lot more than you think he does. Worse, he may [ital] *think* he knows things that just aren't true. To help your comfort level for conversation and discussion, start early, start small, and work your way up. Gauge your topics and conversation through your child's response. Some children are more sensitive than others, and yours will provide clues when uncomfortable. If so, let it go for the moment, but be sure to revisit the topic again soon.

In the early years, begin with the proper names of body parts. This will help in later discussions. Because she could be a victim of such, talk about inappropriate touching. Children as young as four- or five-years-old should learn how to handle a few potentially dangerous situations; most especially what to do if approached by a stranger.

Whether we as parents like it or not, our children always hit puberty. The time to talk about the physical changes that accompany it is before you see the telltale signs. It's also the time to have "the talk" about human reproduction. And while you're on the subject, don't forget about an introduction to STDs and HIV/AIDS and prevention. Yes, the talk may be difficult and uncomfortable, but it sure beats watching your child suffer with the consequences of uninformed, unprotected sex in the future.

As your child grows, and *you* know she's feeling the effects of social and emotional pressures of puberty, it's time to talk in earnest about the disease risk of unhealthy behavior. If you haven't already, take time to talk about conception and pregnancy. With a son, you can emphasize responsibility and the life-altering consequences; with a daughter, ditto, plus. And all should know about the concepts of love, fidelity, and the redeeming qualities of abstinence.

Good decision making skills will not only help your child get ahead in school, but protect his health and well-being. While many of today's parents rely on "experts" such as Dr. Phil and Oprah to tell them what to do, your child can grow learning to think for himself. Help her develop an internal process for analyzing a situation, putting a solution into effect, and one way or another, solving the problem. Independent decision-making is critical to school and personal success. And if you study history with your child, you'll find it's the hallmark of historical greatness.

COACHING TECHNIQUE: REVEAL THE PURPOSE OF EDUCATION

BENEFITS: Promotes enthusiasm and interest, gives rise to a sense of wonder, builds confidence, adds context to learning, increases initiative

For your child, this technique can tie together all the pieces of education with a big red bow. Often the schooling experience presents children with an on-going series of "factlets;" small, mentally digestible pieces of information dispensed on schedule. It can be difficult to impossible to discern the underlying purpose of it all. In school, your child learns a lot of unrelated facts, facts, facts. Homework is answering fact-based questions, and school exercises are based on what facts she can recall. This rote regurgitation of facts is not the true purpose of learning.

As learning coach, your job is not to supplement the education your child receives in school, but rather to enhance it. It isn't to immerse your child in grades, scholastic achievement, gifted classes, skipping grades, joining the National Honor Society, or going all out for some nebulous recognition like being valedictorian. You aren't working to replace the public school system, not unless you really want to get into homeschooling your child, and that's another ball game.

Your job as learning coach is to transcend the school orientation of teaching and convey to your child what the real purpose of education is—and to instill in her the general concepts, principles, and wonder that allow her to solve her own problems and make her way in the world as a competent adult. You are free to take math, science, history, and other school subjects and relate them to your child's world and experience so she has a better understanding of the historical, ethical, and practical problems that she is sure to face.

Eva lived with her husband and son, Timmy, one block from the railroad tracks near the steel mill. She was a high energy, dynamic, intelligent, and conscientious mother who was absolutely determined to make sure her son succeeded in the public school system.

Although the family had little money, Eva began acquiring *every* textbook that Timmy was going to use. She got answer keys to almost every question with which he would be confronted in the coming years in public school—from age six to the end of high school. She made sure Timmy could pass tests, get papers done, and meet every teacher's expectation. She went over every homework assignment, and made sure the boy had the right answer. There was virtually no test, no book report, no math, science, or social studies quiz or test for which Timmy did not get an "A."

It didn't take Timmy long to learn that a "B" was not a good grade.

Often, Eva would keep Timmy home from school to teach him herself. His teachers were astounded, and his classmates hated him. Timmy grew bewildered and flustered. "If I'm an achiever and successful," he wondered, "why are the kids always beating me up at recess because of my grades? Why do they call me Teacher's Pet and Brown Nose?"

Like many of us, Eva made the contemporary mistake of dwelling too much on the school's emphasis on memorizing facts, and not spending enough time on working on instilling an understanding of the basic skills and concepts required to truly succeed in life. Tim later became the high school valedictorian, and was successful in college and graduate school. At this point, after 19 years of schooling, Tim realized he didn't really know very much about life or even for that matter—how to earn a good living. Very little that was studied during those 19 years had any utility for the real world. He knew little about reality, life, love, sex, health, or how to handle a domestic emergency—and he didn't have a good grasp of most life skills.

Tim is retired today, and as he looks back he sees that Eva made some serious mistakes in the way she attempted to be a learning coach. He's forgotten most of what he so diligently memorized so many years ago, but the lesson that remains from the experience has served him well. "Timmy," Eva would tell him, "in the end, whatever the problem is, no matter how tough it gets, you can handle it, you almost always will find the answer, where this is a will there is a way, and you keep at it, quietly and on your own, and you *solve* the problem—without complaining—you just get it done."

Independence, tenacity, self-confidence, and dependability stuck. So despite having been an all-around "A" student who didn't know much about the real world, Tim realized success in the business world.

Tim offers to you the lessons from his experience. "Please defy the status quo and tell your child not to worry about getting the best grades, getting into the Honor Society, being the school's best jock, or always having the correct answer to some irrelevant question. The true purpose of learning is to delegate to your child in such a way that you instill the following traits:

- A sense of wonderment
- An understanding of how his studies have meaning, applicability, and utility in the real world
- An understanding that regurgitating fact after fact is not a mark of learning if she doesn't understand how the concept has meaning in her life
- A sense of personal confidence and independence that allows a child to hold his head high with pride even if he doesn't receive the best grades
- An understanding of the principles of giving, selflessness, generosity, patience, peace, and love"

The life-affirming traits Tim talks about above won't grow overnight, but with your guidance as a learning coach who knows how to delegate responsibility, sets challenging yet reachable goals, prepares your child for independence, and reminds her through words and actions that education is much more valuable than a few test scores, they will blossom and serve your child well.

CHAPTER 9

COACHING TECHNIQUES FOR IMMEDIATE CLASSROOM CHALLENGES

Awareness and understanding of the multiple intelligences and varied learning styles we each possess can help ease at least some of your stress and concern over any classroom difficulties your child may be having. You can remember that no matter how intelligent, nobody is good at everything. A nine year-old math whiz might not be able to spell his way out of a wet paper bag. The early reader might *not* "get" the worm in biology class.

On the other hand, your child's particular intelligences may not be appreciated in the classroom. Perhaps his need-to-touch learning style makes it difficult for him to sit at a desk for extended periods of time. Maybe he's wondering how a rocketship gets into space while the teacher expounds upon the major exports of Argentina.

Problems at school arise for many reasons, most of which have nothing to do with your child's intelligence or ability to learn. The coaching techniques in this chapter, coupled with your understanding of learning styles and different types of intelligence, will help you capitalize on your child's strengths to shore up his weaknesses. You can tackle—and overcome—classroom challenges together.

COACHING TECHNIQUE: FIRST-AID FOR YOUR CHILD'S MIND: BECOME YOUR CHILD'S SHORT-TERM TUTOR

BENEFITS: Improves problem-solving skills, builds understanding of the thinking process, promotes focus

Tucking away a first-aid kit gives you a sense of security and preparedness. It's not something you use daily; it's there in case of emergency, to allow you self-sufficiency in handling physical problems. You can think of short-term tutoring in the same way, except it's for your child's mind. It's not something you would resort to everyday, yet it's at your disposal in case of emergency.

If your child needs immediate help in a particular subject, you can apply an educational "Band-Aid" with short-term tutoring. Address the problem area directly, doing what is necessary to get your child over the present hump, be it homework, a paper, or a pending quiz or test. But don't stop there. Because school studies are incremental, a child can miss one little piece of the puzzle and get stuck or lost. As learning coach, you've learned to observe, and you can put that skill to work here, too.

Mandy, a single mom, noticed that after always doing "OK" with math, over the course of one year her eleven year-old daughter Alycia's grade plummeted. She helped Alycia over the existing hump of multiplying decimals, but then spent a few evenings backtracking through Alycia's textbook with her to get a sense of the big picture. She discovered that Alycia missed a turn before multiplication came into play.

"I knew if she'd missed it the first time around with the textbook, it wouldn't make sense to tutor her with the same book," says Mandy, "so I sat on the Internet for a couple of nights, using the list of skills from the book's table of contents to find different ways of presenting the same information. It was overwhelming," Mandy says, "because there is so much! We began with math.com's section on decimals. By back-tracking through the site's review problems, which Alycia enjoyed much more than her book, I discovered she'd missed the former skills of adding and subtracting decimals. We went back to the beginning and the explanation of place value, and that explained why she was lost—she'd never gotten this. We played with several different Web sites before stumbling on to the mathleague.com's very simple and brief explanation of 'comparing decimal numbers' along with a few examples. That was it—it was like watching a light bulb go on over her head where decimals were concerned. In retrospect, the hardest part was needing to help her keep up with homework she didn't understand every night. Even though we were playing detective to find out where she'd gotten lost, and then had to play 'catch up,' she still had to keep going in the textbook."

Mandy makes an important point. Regardless of the cause, or how confused, lost, or off-track your child may be, the nature of the classroom is that lessons continue in a sequential manner whether or not an individual child has grasped a fact or a concept. Under these circumstances, short-term tutoring, while perhaps the least desirable among your coaching techniques under normal conditions, is the most efficient coaching technique. Indeed, Mandy estimates it took several months of "extra homework" before Alycia began to put enough of the pieces together to improve her grades again. As is usually the case, the solution to the problem wasn't more of the same homework, worksheets, or solving fifty problems instead of twenty (I never could understand why if you couldn't do twenty the teacher would tell you to do fifty . . . but I digress).

You have different mental Band-Aids in your learning coach first-aid kit for other causes of academic problems. Sometimes, it's a personality conflict with the teacher or, I know it's politically incorrect to say this, a bad teacher. It might not be the most pleasant conversation you've ever had, but you need to talk with the teacher to find out. You may need to speak with the principal or superintendent. You may need to get your child placed into a different classroom.

Your child may be experiencing stress, bullying, or other negative emotions, the roots of which need to be uncovered and addressed. If it's a problem of mismatched learning styles, provide lots of chances at home for him to use his strengths, and show him how to use what he does well to help him in the classroom. If she's being tormented with peer comments about being too smart, too stupid, too (whatever), provide opportunities for her to step out of that role, and let her know you accept and support her "as is." As children spend more and more time in school, the odds of plain and simple burn-out increase and your child may be losing interest in the subjects at hand. Learning coach, you make learning fun again.

As an emergency tutor, you will address subjects and topics

directly. Don't forget to use the indirect approach at the same time. When learning coach Cynthia's son refused to study spelling, they both learned radio code (alpha, bravo, Charlie, etc.) and "didn't spell words" with it. Cassie focused on increasing her son's attention span with the riddles and magic tricks he loved, and this improved his reading comprehension. To improve her daughter's math and reading analysis skills, Roxanne turned the game of chess into the family's nightly entertainment.

If you need to tutor, keep the big picture in view. Continue exercising your observation skills, think outside the box for ways to capitalize on your child's learning styles and intelligences, and help him connect the pieces of learning to each other and to the greater world. This will keep your tenure as tutor brief and brilliant.

COACHING TECHNIQUE: THINKING OUT LOUD

BENEFITS: Builds understanding of the thinking process, promotes focus, builds concentration, improves problem-solving skills, improves decision-making skills, builds confidence, adds context to learning

I'll let you in on a secret. This is my favorite coaching technique because, for me, it's the most fun. It was also responsible for some of the best conversations I ever had with my three children as they were growing up. I call it "thinking out loud." My friend, Ann Larhrson Fisher, who unbeknownst to me was practicing the same technique in her home on the other side of the country, called it a much more accurate "mental demonstration" in her book, *Fundamentals of Homeschooling: Notes on Successful Family Living*. It will build your child's confidence at the time he most needs that to cope with the challenges facing him in the classroom.

I stumbled upon this technique by accident. Or maybe, like many other things, you can say my children discovered, or at least helped me, discover it. Confession time: With a mind stuck in overdrive most of the time, I've talked to myself, out loud at times, for as long as I can remember. I also talk to animals, plants, Mother Nature, the radio, the television box, computers, tiny babies, and uncooperative appliances. Once I began learning at home with my children, it wasn't out of the ordinary to talk to educational videos, malfunctioning computer programs, or incomprehensible science experiment directions, either.

I was thrilled to hear that what some might term a strange habit was actually a beneficial one according to Dr. Arnold Scheibel, whose work on the postnatal development of the brain's motor speech area is reported on in Jane Healy's *Endangered Minds: Why Children Don't Think and What We Can Do About It*. No one was more surprised than I to read, "Without being melodramatic, I think it would be very important to tell parents they are participating with the physical development of their youngsters' brains to the degree that they interact with them, communicate with them. Language interaction is actually building tissue in their brains—so it's also helping build youngsters' futures."

Wow, I thought, I could do all that just through this silly little habit that comes so naturally? Not only is this technique fun, it's got to be the simplest and most effective, adaptable to a busy lifestyle way to help your child be a successful learner ever invented—or discovered by accident.

It began innocently enough. I started noticing how frequently, after one of my comments, my children asked, "Why did you say that?" Being ever-alert for learning opportunities, I viewed this question as an invitation to discussion. We could become so engrossed in conversation that oftentimes an hour flew by. Our discussions almost always elicited questions that needed answers.

There is no complicated educational formula here; it only makes sense. What does a learning coach do when she wants to help her child learn how to feed the dog or say I'm sorry? You show him how it's done! Thinking out loud, as well as wondering out loud, show him how to think and wonder. What better way to academic success than possessing this basic skill that can be applied to every school subject, indeed, every aspect of life? Your child practices forming and expressing his opinion, and will appreciate an active role in the family decision-making process, making it ever easier to make the bigger decisions in life.

I learned to think out loud throughout the day, and so can you. It doesn't need to be related to schoolwork; learning happens as part of daily life. "I thought it was awfully nice that the cashier waited so patiently for that elderly couple to pay for their groceries." "I wonder if one pizza will be enough for dinner or if we should order two." "I wonder what I'll find when I dig a hole right here."

Your child will spend a moment considering the cashier's kindness. He'll figure out how many slices of pizza each family member is likely to eat and add them up (probably deciding that two pizzas are best no matter what the final tally). He'll happily join you in digging, observing, and examining what might be lurking in the ground.

Be patient. Tasks may initially take a little longer than if you do them yourself, but patience will be rewarded. "Do we have enough change in our pockets to buy ice cream?" Ann writes in *Fundamentals of Homeschooling*. "Let's see. Ice cream costs seventy-five cents. You have a quarter and a penny. Here is my change. How many more quarters do we need? Here is one, and we still need another. A quarter is worth twenty-five cents. Let's see if we can make that value with these dimes and pennies." You let your child know there is no big mystery to the process of counting change and making purchases. Later, when he begins to grasp these ideas, he can take them over for you when you haul out your fistful of change."

With a young child, spice things up and throw in a touch of silliness. (You can do this with teenagers, too, just to check to see if they're listening.) "The car is awfully dirty. I think I'll put it in the washing machine." It makes your child giggle, you do it as a matter of course while you continue your activity (no need to stop, sit down, and get all serious), and in a relaxed way it gets her thinking about why things are the way they are, figuring out the world she so innately wishes to understand.

Think and wonder aloud about everything. Encourage your child to do the same. Look forward to the day, when you least expect it, to be outwitted or out-debated by that same child you used to make giggle about cars in dishwashers.

COACHING TECHNIQUE: PARAPHRASE

BENEFITS: Builds confidence, adds context to learning, promotes focus, builds understanding of the thinking process

A friend tells you a story. It seems so incredible that you say, "Wait a minute. Are you telling me that . . ." In order to make sure you got the story straight, you just paraphrased. You might do the same when someone at work asks you to perform a series of tasks. We do this to double-check and make sure we've understood what someone has told us. It's a proven method to ensure we have received communicated information properly.

At times, classroom challenges arise because your child is having difficulty receiving communicated information properly. If this is the case, make sure it's not a hearing or vision problem. Check with the teacher to ascertain it isn't simply that he's not paying attention. It's difficult for anyone to process information within the classroom while dreaming about flying with the birds outside the window. If you rule these out, by engaging in two-way paraphrasing with his learning coach at home he can sharpen his information-processing skills so they work more quickly and naturally in the classroom.

At the beginning, many learning coaches find it helps to speak a bit slower. In addition, they help their students by providing information in the form that best matches innate intelligence. Whether your child remembers best by hearing (auditory), seeing (visual), or reading (sequential), use this knowledge to deliver information in the way that makes it easiest for him to receive it. Talk with his teacher about your discovery and enlist her aid.

Arlene marveled at the breadth of the benefits of paraphrasing. In fifth grade her twelve year-old daughter, Sonja, began having difficulty in the classroom. Arlene arranged with the teacher to sit in class one day to try to get to the bottom of it. "I saw Sonja listen intently to the instructions given to the class by the teacher," says Arlene, "then noticed she kept looking around at what everyone else was doing. I questioned her about it when we were on our way home. Sonja explained that she couldn't remember, so looked at the other kids for 'clues' as to what she was supposed to do."

Arlene spent the next week paraphrasing what Sonja told her in discussions to model the behavior. The next week she told her daughter to do the same for her. "Sonja found this very difficult at first, so we started slowly, often just one sentence at a time. I'd say something like, 'On the way home we have to stop at the pet store for dog food, pick up a newspaper, and let's talk about what you'd like for dinner because we have to get that, too. So what are we off to do?'"

Arlene showed Sonja how to "whisper to herself" to remember the important points. She suggested creating mental pictures or making associations (such as an apple to remember Mr. Applebaum's name) which Sonja could draw upon when it came time to paraphrase. At dinner and throughout the evening Arlene would share stories of her day, then ask Sonja to summarize each. As the girl did any homework reading, she'd stop to paraphrase a paragraph or section. In the meantime, Arlene kept paraphrasing, too, providing an ever-present role model.

"We went full speed ahead for about two months," Arlene explains, "and now it's what you might call maintenance. She still doesn't remember everything, but she remembers a heck of a lot more than she used to, and her teacher has noticed the improvement, as well. Three other results are equally important, though," adds Arlene. "First is the giant leap we took in communicating with each other. We understand each other so much better. I can see how we used to talk 'at' each other; now we talk 'to' each other and have grown closer because of it. Second is that by my practicing this skill in the greater world I can see an improvement in my communications at large, resulting in far fewer misunderstandings. And last but not least is that Sonja's self-confidence has grown right along with her memory. The person I'm getting to know better is rapidly changing from a timid girl into a self-assured young lady. That's the most beautiful part."

COACHING TECHNIQUE: CHALLENGE AND CHEERLEAD YOUR CHILD TO GREATER HEIGHTS

BENEFITS: Builds confidence, increases self-responsibility, improves decision-making skills, improves problem-solving skills, increases initiative, builds concentration

If your child is facing classroom challenges, chances are he's not exactly feeling as good about himself as he is capable of feeling. If left unchecked, a negative sense of self-worth can make a bad situation worse and cause it to spiral out of control. But just as a negative sense can feed on itself, so can a positive one. You need only plant the seed of positivity, then water, nurture, and support it in every way you can. Learning coaches find that a two-pronged approach—challenge and cheerleading—works well to rebuild confidence and the initiative to do well. But first, learning coach, you have to do *your* homework.

Every problem (or pesky weed) has a root. And all the positive nurturing in the world isn't going to help if you don't first get that weed out of the way. Older children are capable of explaining, or at least giving you enough clues to help you figure out, the problem at school. Encourage the habit of keeping a journal, a tool many have found dispels confusion, worry, and anger while at the same time acting as a vehicle of self-discovery, uncovering wisdom and insight one may not have realized she possesses. You may ask to read the journal, but don't invade the privacy and freedom of expression represented by it without permission. Younger ones may need a little encouragement. Enlist the aid of all the suggestions throughout this book, and add role play to your repertoire. If applicable to your child, try it with favorite stuffed animals or dolls who may speak for her. Simply get down on the floor with your child and begin playing with them. Lead the conversation around to "let's play school," and let the inanimate objects take the leading roles. Use your observation skills to watch for clues as your child takes on various roles (not necessarily in the same round of play). He can alternately be the student, the teacher, the mean kid, the nice friend, the smart kid, the dumb kid. Follow his lead—and the clues he provides. If appropriate and it won't cause your child to shut down, include other family members, especially your spouse, in supporting roles.

Oh, the woes of a child attending school. The root might be strictly academic as discussed elsewhere. But it could be one or more other children making fun of his name, his teeth, his ears. Perhaps her emphasis on comfortable clothing doesn't mirror what classmates think is fashionable (especially true for girls). The class/bus/school bully may have found your child to be the perfect target. Classmates may think he's too fat, too skinny, too clumsy, too smart, too dumb—the "too" list could go on forever. She may not like the teacher(s), feel she's not liked by them, or have suffered the indignity of public humiliation. Whatever the weed, encourage your child to bring it to the fore so you may effectively pull it out.

Begin rebuilding your child's sense of worth at the same time. When, through much conversation, Laura discovered that her twelve year-old son, Aiden's, academic problems were likely a result of the consequences of an on-going weight problem, she first spoke with the teacher, teacher's aide, and principal, requesting that they keep a closer eye on the taunting that was occurring both in and out of the classroom. "They did a fairly competent job of it," says Laura, "but my job was far from over. We implemented a family-wide diet and exercise change under the supervision of our family doctor. But I still had to help Aiden feel better about himself and his competence—a kid doesn't need to get too many 'Ds' before he starts thinking he's stupid." Instead of watching for what Aiden was doing wrong, Laura and Mike, her husband, jointly agreed to a team effort to catch Aiden "doing something right."

"He's a conscientious kid so it was pretty easy," Mike says. "Whether it was a little thing, like letting the cat out without being asked, or a bigger one, like keeping an eye on his little sister for an entire weekend while his mom finished a big work project, we took the time to say thank you, let him know how helpful he'd been, and tell him he'd done an excellent job of it. To be honest, I felt badly that it took us this long to say things so easy and simple yet so utterly important."

Brainstorming about what challenges they could present Aiden with to help him stretch higher, the couple kept coming back to his natural knack for math, so "we explained to him how busy we are with our home business and told him we could use some help," says Laura. "Mike taught him how to balance our checking accounts, and gave him an unused register to practice, in which Mike and I would write pretend transactions, and Mike created statements for his review. He did so well we asked if he thought he could handle the challenge of more responsibility—he was thrilled. Mike and I both keep car mileage logs that regularly need to be filled in and tallied. I showed him how to follow our stocks on the computer so he could give us a report every few days. He tackled how to track our inventory and create a monthly order list. He's learning how to keep our accounting books now."

Mike responds, "Aiden's happier, healthier (well, we *all* are, he adds), his homework is impeccable, we haven't heard a complaint about school in months, and his grades are improving. The kid was truly suffering."

"He rose to every challenge," Laura says, "and the only one prouder of him than Mike and me is Aiden."

It's best to tackle any problem head-on, and the same goes for learning coaches dealing with their children's immediate classroom challenges. Keep in mind that while handling them may take your attention away from the greater learning picture for a time, you can continue your normal learning coach activities, or return to them when the problem is under control. Play, talk, explore, read, question, be together—these remain your best tools to guide your child in successful learning.

CHAPTER 10

THE THREE ESSENTIAL SOURCES FOR INDEPENDENT INQUIRY

Congratulations! You've come a long way in understanding the difference between teaching and coaching, multiple intelligences and learning styles, the habit of observation, coaching techniques, and, most importantly, that wonderful, unique, and precious child for whom you want to open up a lifetime of enjoyable education. You realize that learning has depth and breadth that transcend school buildings if only we take advantage of the potential lessons residing within every task we perform, every person we meet, every insect, flower, or rock we encounter as we go about daily life.

Empowered by this knowledge, you step into the world of independent inquiry. That is, you leave behind the constraints of the school's schedule, methods, and organization that dictate what, when, and in how much depth your child will study something.

Along with the freedom from these constraints comes the responsibility of knowing where and how to get just as much good information as necessary for yourself, as well as show your child how to do so. Learning coaches find that not only are the three best sources wonderfully inexpensive, they're also readily available. Let's visit them now.

TECHNOLOGY

While you can certainly have a good time and do a great job as learning coach without it, today's technology goes a long way in supporting your efforts. Think of your computer, television, and videos and DVDs as vehicles directly delivering into your home the information you want, when and how you want it.

The "Other" Screened Box

Do you remember life before personal computers? Today's children sure won't. In fact, a January, 2005, Associated Press article reports that U.S. schools are behind in technology, noting that "students of almost any age are far ahead of their teachers in computer literacy," according to a U.S. Education Department report on school technology that "is based on comments from thousands of students, teachers, administrators, and education groups. Students say they see this knowledge gap daily."

Since the computer has become part of life in the twenty-first century and shows no sign of disappearing, it makes sense that your child should grow up viewing and using it as the powerful learning tool it is. And as "schools lag behind much of society in using technology," according to the government report, it's vital to fill in the gaps at home. If you don't have a computer and feel you can't afford one, head to your library where computers with Internet access are almost universally available. A librarian can quickly show you enough basics to get you on to the Internet where you can look for lower cost, refurbished models, or check out online auctions, such as eBay (www.ebay.com), where every day both individuals and businesses auction off to the highest bidder computers that they've replaced with more modern counterparts. If that's still too steep for your budget, reach into your time pocket, instead, and plan on a weekly trip (at least) to the library with your protégée, and use one of those computers to accomplish your learning goals.

THE INTERNET

Where once parents used to tell children, "Go look it up in the encyclopedia" (and you had to hope that "it" could be found), today's parent exhorts a child to "go look it up on the Internet" where there's a much better chance he'll find what he's looking for.

Indeed, there is so much available that you as learning coach could make a career out of researching what you want. If you don't have time for a second career, head down to your favorite bookstore where shelves are teeming with help on the subject, including *You are Here: Kids and Family Internet Guide* by Eric Labow, *How to Find Almost Anything on the Internet: A Kids' Guide to Safe Surfing* by Ted Pederson, *Stay Safe in Cyberspace: Kids' Guide* by Victoria Roddel, and for you, *A Parent's Guide to the Internet* by Ilene Raymond.

You'll find on the Net that entire text of books old and new await your attention, and need only to be downloaded and printed, some free, some not. Your child could make a protective cover all his own. Need a dictionary, encyclopedia, thesaurus, atlas, language translator, song lyric, or world atlas? No problem. Want a unit study, lesson plans, skills-specific worksheets, art and music activities, or science experiments? They're all there, many for free. If it happens to be a sticking point for you, many of the free materials are thinly disguised advertisements for products or points of view. Be sure to check for this "syndrome" before you waste your own paper and ink to print them out. The Internet is indeed a thriving marketplace, so for a fee you can also get online classes, tutorials, or consulting services, or an entire curriculum (though I don't know why you'd want one with all the fascinating ways to go about learning without such a product).

Modern technology has truly created an information super highway. Let it take you and your child wherever curiosity and interest lead.

FAVORITE EDUCATIONAL WEBSITES OF THE AGES 3-12 CROWD

American Girl: americangirl.com

The American Girl series (titled American Girls Collection) is a set of stories by a variety of authors told through the eyes of young girls living in different time periods. This site gives more on the stories, has a fan club, magazine, and more.

Barbie: everythinggirl.com

Falling at least a little short of "everything girl," four main links for games, fashion, friends, and arts and crafts.

Between the Lions: pbskids.org/lions

The award-winning show's Web site provides stories, games, things to print, songs, a newsletter, recommends books, and provides a special link for parents and teachers.

Country Reports: countryreports.org

Choose from a list of over 260 countries for a map and "quick facts" (everything your social studies teacher wishes you would know). Subscribe for $10/year for "expanded" information, a country holiday calendar, translations of common phrases, and national anthem lyrics.

Crayola: crayola.com

Coloring in the twenty-first century at its finest. Kids get a game room, arts and crafts, e-card creator, color corner, and a coloring and activity section. Parents get tips on communicating with their children's schools, traveling with kids, party fun, and simple ways to bring creativity into the home.

Cyber Kids: cyberkids.com

Among that which is "hot" at Cyber Kids is the Learning Center. And while it may not be hot, you might like to click where it says, "Parents click here."

Discovery: discovery.com

Yes, you'll find the popular television show's schedule, but there's also "Discovery Kids," where a chamber of mystery, yucky games, and Kenny the Shark are teeming with lessons.

Disney: disney.com

Choose from among the colorful, pure Disney fun areas of Playhouse, Disney Blast, Toontown Online, Kids Island (music, games and more) and Family Fun, full of crafts, recipes, and "boredom busters."

ESPN: ESPN.COM

If your sports fan doesn't find it here, then it probably didn't happen.

Harry Potter:

http://www.scholastic.com/harrypotter/home.asp

Fun for fans of all ages—from a preschool playground to games and contests, discussion lists, a club for kids who love books, and homework help in the form of current event quizzes, reading comprehension, how to "master multiple choice" and more.

History Channel: historychannel.com

Kids Learning Zone: kids-learning-zone.com

Courtesy of Sylvan, the learning center folks, online help in reading and math from preschool to ninth grade.

Legos: legos.com

Visit Legolands around the world, join the club and enter contests, play multi-player games, and build your own Lego Web page; and of course you can shop.

National Gallery of Art: nga.gov

Check out upcoming events, take an online tour, and visit NGA-Kids for homework help, activities and projects, and interesting, hands-on links, such as 3-D Traveler (explore the third dimension), Cubits (construct a geometric sculpture), and Collage Machine.

National Zoo: nationalzoo.si.edu/default.cfm

Everything animals! Take a Web-cam tour, delve into study topics, meet world record animals, peruse the photo gallery, and learn about ecosystems, protection, and conservation.

Nick Jr.: nickjr.com

"Play to learn" with favorites like Blue's Clues, Dora the Explorer, Little Bill and more. Watch stories online, get play-together ideas, and cooking, craft, and sports activities, even yoga for preschoolers.

Nickelodeon: nick.com

For kids who graduate from Nick Jr., games, puzzles, arcade, message boards, and fun attention to topics like nutrition and online safety.

Nintendo: nintendoland.com

Read the complete history of Nintendo, play online games, and learn all about Mario. Plenty of reviews, game secrets, fan fiction, message boards for discussion and commerce, and funny facts.

PBS: pbs.com

Stay abreast of upcoming features, get parenting advice, and access learning materials for teachers.

Save the Manatee Club: savethemanatee.org

Everything you ever wanted to know about manatees, including how to adopt one.

Sea World: seaworld.com

Visit Sea World locations in Orlando, San Diego, and San Antonio to find educational resources and online fun that often involves Shamu.

Sesame Street: sesameworkshop.com

The perennial favorite offers games and parenting tips, healthy habits for life, and free newsletter.

Thomas the Tank Engine: hitentertainment.com/thomasandfriends

Start by clicking on your country's flag and you're off to the Island of Sodor and games, activities, programming information and news, and shopping.

SOFTWARE

What do you get when you combine brilliant graphics, fun basic premises and/or characters, the ability to receive immediate feedback, and educational material? Interesting learning via software, that's what! If you're coaching a younger child, software is often more appropriate and definitely more controllable than the Internet. An added bonus, it's usually set up to satisfy the attention span of a younger child, too.

Again, offerings are so numerous as to require books and constantly updated reviews, so suffice it to say that you *will* find fun, educational software connected to your child's main interests, usually in the form of a game and often accompanied by the presence of trademark licensed "personalities" (such as Bert and Ernie, my personal, perennial favorites). It's a large market to keep track of, and of course some programs are much better than others, so use one or several of the Internet software review sites available to help save you money. Here are a few locations to get you started.

- childrenssoftware.com
- superkids.com
- the reviewzone.com
- edutaining kids.com
- computingwithkids.com
- gzkidzone.com

Software covers every school subject area, but there's no need to stop there. You and your child can delve into foreign languages, or explore what it's like to write, direct, and perform with a theater company with the Opening Night CD. "What I like best about software," explains learning coach Maria, "is that you can stock up on reference materials without turning your home into a maze of bookshelves. It's all there on CDs just waiting to be used. And it is."

COMPUTER CAVEATS

As with everything else in life, computers offer the temptation of getting "too much of a good thing." As a repository of information about *everything*, it also holds much you wouldn't want your child to see. Many learning coaches supervise the entirety of their children's surfing time. If your child will spend any amount of time on the Internet without adult supervision, check if your Internet service provider (ISP) offers any parent controls and ask for assistance in using them, if necessary. You might consider purchasing one of the many filtering programs that allows you to restrict from your child's view that which you find inappropriate or offensive, such as:

- Cyber Patrol: www.cyberpatrol.com
- Cyber Sitter: www.cybersitter.com
- Net Mop: www.netmop.com
- Net Nanny: www.netnanny.com
- Off the Computer: www.offthecomputer.com (sets time limits)
- Safety Surf: www.safetysurf.com
- Surf Control: www.surfcontrol.com

As learning coach you not only need to be concerned with what your child sees on the computer, but also with how much time he spends seeing it. Long-term effects of use, including concerns about radiation exposure, are still unknown. Optometrists report an increase in the number of patients complaining of computer vision syndrome, that which the American Optometric Association (AOA) defines as a "complex of eye and vision problems related to near work experienced during, or related to, computer use." Visual stress symptoms include headaches, eyestrain, and near-sightedness.

Researchers studying repetitive stress injuries, symptoms of which include sore wrists, tingling fingers, and aching back, found that the equipment and its placement are often mismatched to the size of children, causing them to work with craned necks, hunched shoulders, and flexed wrists.

Then there's the potential for your child to spend so much time at the keyboard as to neglect necessary, vigorous exercise. Like many other learning coaches, Marta highly recommends using a timer to set limits. "With a timer, all three of my kids know they're getting equal time, and there's no fuss about 'a few more minutes' anymore. The buzzer became the authority, one they can't sweet talk."

Author and reading specialist Pat Wyman also notes that playing catch, riding a bike, and participating in sports strengthens crucial reading abilities such as tracking, peripheral vision, focusing, eye teaming, and eye-hand coordination, while improving near- and far-point vision.

KIDS AND COMPUTERS: CAUTIONARY MEASURES

- When your child is not on the computer, encourage him to engage in robust physical activity.
- Encourage frequent breaks, at least ten out of every thirty minutes for younger children.

- Provide appropriate furniture.
- Help your child establish the habits of proper posture, keyboard technique, and looking up from the computer every few minutes to focus on something in the distance.
- Add a wrist support to the keyboard; teach your child when and when not to use it.
- Make sure your child's face and eyes are at least twenty to twenty-six inches away from the screen.
- Position screen so the center is about four to nine inches below eye level.
- Purchase a micro-mesh filter for added protection.
- Eliminate glare on the screen by modifying room lighting or position of computer relative to lighting.
- Set monitor controls at maximum contrast and moderate brightness.

The Original Screened Box

I've had a love/hate relationship with the original screened box, commonly known as the television, since having my first child. On one hand, it's filled with mind-numbing programming that can waste time quicker than counting the stalks in a haystack. On the other hand, educational gems pop up like needles in that stack, and it would be a shame to miss them. The same goes for videotapes and DVDs which free us to view the good stuff on our own schedules. Many learning coaches find that the original screened box is a useful tool, noting its visual and auditory appeal and ability to capture the attention of a child who learns best in these ways.

"My son is fascinated by cultural differences," says Naomi of eight year-old Ethan. "We can't afford the real thing, so we 'travel' the world through *National Geographic* shows on videotape. Our library houses a great collection that includes a lot of 'freebies' from travel bureaus, so we check these out, too. They feed his imagination while inspiring him to think in terms of exploration when he's older."

Roberta, whose daughters are ten and twelve, uses the original screened box to support their history studies. "I hit the library, then the video store, to find a good movie set in the time period they're about to study," she says. "We watch for and talk about clothing, food, accents and ways of speaking, attitudes toward children, women, minorities, anything that helps them 'connect.' When they think in terms of history as people, they're definitely more inter-ested, and it helps them get through what is oftentimes a pretty boring rendition of the times in their text books." The same, learn-ing coaches have discovered, holds true when tackling Shakespeare to advancing math, and everything in-between.

Karla capitalizes on her three children's interest in animals. She rents several educational videos about them each month, but also combs her TV program guide each week to make sure the family catches any-thing of interest. "It's well worth the little bit of time it takes," she explains. "They watch because of the featured animal, of course. But at the same time they learn about the environment, geography, history, climate, and nontraditional jobs related to science. When our sched-ule allows, I also try to pick up an interesting book about the animal, preferably one written by a scientist. Even the youngest," Karla adds, "who is six, sits still for these read-alouds."

Public television and cable channels offer a plethora of educational programming. Learning coaches record programming and hang on to it in anticipation of the child's future studies, or to avoid developing the habit of sitting down in front of the TV at regular intervals, and create an inexpensive video library of their own. "Just be sure," advises learning coach Jacqueline, "to break off that little tab on the back if the program is important. When my son is excited about capturing a program on lions, he doesn't check to see if there may already be something saved on the tape. I lost programs on the Space Shuttle and the Civil War before I learned to do this." If you can't find anything on a topic your child is interested in, look it up on the Internet or write to organizations that specialize in that field. They often offer videos in catalogs of their wares.

The key to effective use of technology is balance. Watch the amount of time, type of use, and life priority currently given to it, and weigh the benefits against repercussions. Make adjustments accordingly. Think of technology as a tool available when needed, and it will stay in its place while still serving as a gateway to a world's worth of resources and exploration.

LIBRARIES

After a long day in school, a visit to the library can be a breath of fresh air for your child. Here, no one forces her to read about something in which she's not interested, or says he can't learn about this or that simply because he's the wrong age. Learning coaches quickly discover that the librarians who manage this bastion of free inquiry are great supporting personnel for their learning teams.

If you're not already intimately familiar with what your public library has to offer, I highly recommend you and your child set aside at least a couple of hours to go check it out in detail.

Especially if you live in a large city, call ahead and ask if a librarian can take the time to give you "the grand tour." Be sure to speak with the children's librarian, but talk with other personnel as well. Many of the available resources aren't as obvious as the books, magazines, video, and audiotapes on the shelves. Along with satisfying your child's particular needs, ask if any of the following are also available for your independent inquiry:

- Games, microscopes, puzzles, software
- Microfiche or other collections of old newspapers and magazines
- Space to display your child's projects or artwork
- Recommended reading lists, by subject, age, grade, or otherwise
- Local history collection
- Art collection
- Potential to sign out books for a longer period of time

Ask if the library hosts lectures, workshops, or other programs, and/or if they announce new acquisitions. If they send out announcements or produce a regular newsletter, get on their mailing list. If there's a particular book or magazine subscription you'd like to see the library hold, make a formal request. It would help if you could get a few other families to do the same. Utilize the interlibrary loan capability, a reciprocal relationship among cooperating libraries through which they share their materials, when your child requires resources that your own library doesn't have on hand. Libraries exist to serve the needs of the community, and they can only do so effectively when you make the personnel aware of what your needs are.

While the public library will likely become your primary source of borrowed materials, especially before your child becomes a teen, don't forget to check into other libraries as need might dictate. Many public and private college and university libraries extend privileges to local residents. All institutions, research centers, think tanks, and organizations of every stripe physically reside somewhere, and they, too, maintain interestingly stocked libraries. Residents of the community may receive borrowing privileges here, too. All you need do is ask.

COACH'S MOTIVATIONAL MINUTE: Keep a spiral or other notebook at hand and label it "Library Books." When you hear of a book, read a review, or receive a recommendation that sounds interesting, write down the title and take the notebook with you on the next trip to the library. You could also use this notebook to record titles and due dates of books you checked out. You can note dates of interlibrary loan requests so you can follow up on them, if need be. Your child can use the same list to maintain a running review of books read, perhaps rating each title on a scale of one to five stars, for example. Older children might add a sentence-length summary and brief commentary.

Utilizing all available libraries lets your child stretch toward independence, follow interests to increasing depths, experience the thrill of discovery, and build the skills of research she'll need one day. Interesting, isn't it, that research is often termed "curiosity, formalized."

YOUR COMMUNITY

Learning coach, here's another observation exercise for you. For the next week or so, put your "learning happens everywhere, all the time" perspective into high gear as you're out and about in your community. You just may view the very same places and people you've seen every day for years in a new light.

"Field Trips"

You don't need to wait for the teacher to take your child on interesting, educational field trips. They're a wonderful way to integrate learning while spending time together as a family on weekends, vacations, and during summer break.

Where the concept of museum used to conjure up pure dullness, many museums today cater to the needs of children. Hands-on, interactive exhibits and short demonstrations abound. Not only do they present information your child needs to know in an alternative format, they can spark interest in topics where it didn't previously exist. From nature to art to science, from quirky little specialty exhibitions to mega-institutions, your neighborhood houses *some* place that would be both fun and educational to visit.

You needn't limit yourself to museums, not when there are so many educational venues just waiting to be explored. Historical sites abound, and you'll be amazed at what you don't know about "your own backyard." For most folks there is a state park or forest within day-trip driving distance. Small towns and large cities alike host everything from heritage and history days to festivals celebrating the area's food crops or natural resources. You don't need to participate in a canoe or sailing race to cheer on your favorite entrant. Pay attention to the community calendar in the newspaper, and open your mind to the idea that anything and anywhere is always a potential field trip.

Lend a Hand

It's never too early to cultivate the habit of giving back to one's community, and doing it early lets your child see it as just a civic responsibility, not something for which he should be patted on the head each time. With younger children, include them in any volunteer work in which you already participate. My youngest chose to help at our town's food pantry. At first he only needed to be there for less than an hour as his function was to dismantle and discard empty boxes at the end of the day. As he grew both older and wiser in the ways of the food pantry, and those in charge got to know and trust him, it became an entire afternoon activity as he helped from start to finish.

Your immediate neighborhood offers many chances for individual altruism, even for younger children. Could an elderly neighbor use help with yard work, or a pair of young legs to run to the grocery store for a few items? The family that just moved in or just had a baby would welcome a ready-made meal. How about a babysitter for the young couple who never seems to get a chance to go out, with you just a phone call away, of course? The dog groomer might appreciate someone who can once a week simply sweep the floor. Self-employed, work-at-home folks never have enough time to water the plants, take out the trash, or rake the yard; do any live in your neighborhood?

Behind the Scenes

Often we criticize children for taking for granted all the amenities afforded them by modern society. Yet equally as often we're guilty of failing to help them see all that must be done to provide these amenities. Even if they don't ask, they very well may be wondering how the mail gets in your box each day, or how the local news is broadcast every evening. It's fun to check out what goes on "behind the scenes." Remember, learning is strengthened by connections, and what better way to help your child make them than to expose the pieces that make up the whole picture, the one we are all guilty of taking for granted from time to time. The good news is that children wonder about the simplest things, like mail and news programs, and these types of forays into the community usually take no more than an hour to accomplish with people who are often happy and proud to have their work appreciated.

People

In the end, a community would be nothing without the vast array of people who populate it. Invite and encourage the variety of people

QUICK, EASY, AND FUN
BEHIND THE SCENES "HOT SPOTS"

- Post Office
- Newspaper office
- Community or Commercial Airport
- Bank

- Florist
- Architect's office
- Farm
- Factory
- Hospital
- State forest

- Fish hatchery
- Firehouse
- Police station
- City Hall/ Courthouse
- Television station

you know to share their knowledge and skills with your child. Sure, you can visit their places of work, or as an alternative you can encourage a more personal, one-to-one get-together by inviting such folks for conversation over coffee, dinner, or a barbecue on Sunday afternoon. Please don't ever forget the storehouse of knowledge that resides within your child's grandparents and their friends. Welcome them into your lives as fellow team players who also care deeply about your child's race toward independence and adulthood.

Interesting, creative people live next door and around the corner. Being a learning coach responsible for introducing your child to independent inquiry requires you to look at your community as a microcosm of the great, wide world and take advantage of everything it—and the people who live and work there—has to offer. When you see the wide world as the amazing classroom it is, there are no limits to fun, effective learning for your child.

CHAPTER 11

CREATING A LEARNING COOPERATIVE FOR (OR, WITH!) YOUR CHILD

Perhaps it's because of the media stereotype of homeschoolers sitting around a kitchen table piled with textbooks all day that few outside of the community know about a very successful learning approach that many of them create and participate in. They're called, among other things, learning cooperatives, learning clubs, or learning groups. Similar in philosophy to the food co-ops that sprung up and slowly grew starting twenty to thirty years ago, participants reap the benefits of being a group by holding down costs through shared work.

Learning cooperatives are popular because they're relatively easy, inexpensive, lots of fun, and very, very flexible, which means you can create anything to fill the unique needs or interests of your protege. In addition, cooperatives provide social opportunities outside of a classroom setting. Because they're based on members' common interests or needs, cooperatives can open doors to new friendships and networking opportunities.

Think of Brownies, Cub Scouts, or 4-H. Now take away the huge organizations behind them, replace that with local control (i.e., parents of participants and participants), and you've got a good idea about what learning cooperatives are.

HOW LEARNING COOPERATIVES WORK

It may seem a bit intimidating to start a group without the support of organizations that back the Scouts or 4-H. This, however, is the learning cooperative's strength because the very absence of a controlling organization provides the versatility and flexibility you need to make the group whatever you want it to be. Because of this flexibility, many cooperatives evolve over time, changing as the group learns through experience or as the needs of its members dictate. Many have limited life spans as members come and go, interests change, or when the co-op has served its purpose for at least a majority of members.

COACH'S MOTIVATIONAL MINUTE: Co-ops can be as formal or informal as the creators and participants like. Informal works best with the young crowd, especially since as coaches our goal is to inject fun and hands-on experience into the process. While it's certainly possible to charge full speed ahead on your own, at least consider enlisting the aid of a friend or acquaintance whose child would be interested in the same co-op. Not only will you cut your workload by half, you and a co-coordinator can keep each other motivated, on schedule, and excited by talking about the project.

Like any other gathering of diverse personalities, a co-op needs a sensible purpose. Spend a bit of time thinking about "the perfect learning co-op" for your child. What will the group do, and why? "Bi-weekly weekend get-togethers for seven- to ten-year olds for fun with science." "Informal lessons one night a week for six weeks for children, ages eight to twelve, interested in learning how to sew." "Calling all Lego fanatics, ages five to ninety-five. Let's meet weekly for a month and build something huge!"

Give yourself enough time between the inception of the idea and the actual starting date to "spread the word." You need time to garner support, yet you can't put it off too far into the future or your child may lose interest waiting around for the fun to begin. Create a "must register by" date approximately two weeks in advance of the beginning of the activity so you can make final preparations with a firm number of attendees in mind. A "must register by" date also keeps others from postponing commitment.

When your vision for the co-op is clear you can easily explain it to others. You may be able to gather the size group you want strictly by word-of-mouth (so be sure to tell everyone who will stand still and listen!), but plan on advertising, too. Your clear vision serves as a terrific classified ad in your local freebie newspaper. It can become a short press release sent to the community activity editor of your newspaper, local access cable television station, and radio stations. It's also the meat of a flyer you can hang around town in places frequented by parents who have children of similar ages. Good locations include, but are certainly not limited to, libraries, toy stores, museums, educational supply stores, bookstores, parks, nature, gymnastic, dance, and art centers, children's clothing stores, other specialty shops, supermarkets, and convenience stores. A flyer that includes "tear-off" phone numbers at the bottom is an easy way for busy, rushed parents to take your contact information home with them.

Be sure to gather information from potential participants when they call, too. You'll need name of parent(s), name and age of child(ren), address, phone numbers (work, home, and cell), and email addresses (work, home, and any other). Email can be a real time-saver when you need to get information to all parties quickly, such as when weather forces cancellation of a meeting, there's a change in meeting place or time, or you just remembered something they should bring with them. You can use an informal list of participants' email addresses, but keep in mind participants might like to contact the group from time to time with questions or conversation. A free Yahoo! email group you can set up in minutes by going to www.yahoogroups.com can be valuable. While you're there, you might want to check out existing education-related or subject-specific groups—there are thousands!

You'll want to assemble some guidelines or rules to share with participants from the get-go. Think about how many people constitute an interesting yet manageable group. The purpose or theme you have in mind will help dictate this decision. With children up to age ten or so, it's often best to think in terms of "one per year old," i.e., 5 five-year olds, 6 six-year olds, etc. If there are costs for facilities or instructor, you may also need to think in terms of a minimum number of participants to proceed in order to keep per family costs reasonable. You may want to consider allowing adult participants, as well, depending on the actual ages of the children and the activities involved.

Think in advance about duration of both meetings and the activity itself. If you're doing this on weeknights, forty-five to sixty minute meetings will be about all everyone can handle. You can stretch this if you meet on Saturday mornings or afternoons, or during the summer when there's no school schedule to worry about. You should also create a definite finish date of the activity. If there happens to be unanimous accord to just keep going with the current set-up, great. But families who signed up with an understanding that they'd get the whole enchilada, so to speak, could become very upset if they feel they are missing out by stopping attendance as originally planned. Better to stop, tweak any problems, and start again, even as early as two weeks into the future. This provides the originally promised closure to the first run while still allowing those interested to keep going.

How might responsibilities be doled out? This is essential, because if the group is successful it will likely require more work and time. While it may seem simplest to do it yourself at the beginning, you don't want that to become the norm. Responsibilities need to be spread out so you (or others) don't become so burdened with "doing everything" that family or other obligations suffer. This is the quickest way to kill enjoyment and can lead to burn-out. Oftentimes the chores associated with a learning cooperative can be divvied up simply by putting one person in charge of obtaining meeting space, another in charge of the phone or email tree, yet another making sure necessary supplies are purchased, etc. Another effective method is to have different families in charge of everything for one meeting. This works especially well if you will rotate meetings in members' homes, and you can continue long enough to give everyone a turn.

You'll want to consider who should attend the meetings. Can you or another handle all the children alone? Should a parent attend with the child? If parents stay, what will be required of them? Might it be a "whole family" affair? What about families with babies or toddlers—can the wee ones stay or are other arrangements necessary? Once again, the group's purpose will lend clues to a proper decision about the matter.

Will there be "at home work" associated with the co-op? If so, approximately how much time will it take? While it would be nice to think that once inspired the children will go home and work for hours on a new project, the reality is that most families live on very tight schedules and requiring too much "at home work" could prevent them from participating. Think about this ahead of time so that you can provide a realistic appraisal. In this way parents know just what they're getting into from the start, saving misunderstandings or bad feelings later.

If you're thinking about having a "class" in something, please take time to think again. It's a rare child who has been in class(es) all day who wants yet another at the end of his long day. While the purpose of a co-op is for learning, it's not to add more schooling. If you're short on creative ideas, enlist some help. Check out library books, such as *The Ultimate Book of Homeschooling Ideas: 500+ Fun and Creative Learning Activities for Kids Ages 3-12* by yours truly and others. Go online and search terms such as "unit studies" and "hands-on activities." Whatever you do, don't forget to ask your child what she would like!

Remember that the key word is flexibility, and this should apply to your schedule, too. Go ahead and plan a few activities for each session, but remember that no one is cracking a whip saying you absolutely **must** cover them just because you thought you would or should. There's a strong possibility participants could get really involved in something. Let them! You can always get to the other activities another time. On the other hand, you might plan three activities you believe will fill your meeting hour, only to find nobody is really interested in them and you're all done in twenty-five minutes! You probably won't hear too many complaints if there's a lot of time to play.

Speaking of flexibility, make sure it applies to attendance, too. You're not setting up a school with compulsory attendance rules. Attendance should be strictly voluntary. Yes, this does open the door to people leaving right in the middle of everything, but forced attendance is antithetical to the cooperation necessary to make this concept work. In addition, forced attendance doesn't allow children to experience the self-confidence, self-direction, and goal achievement that are essential outcomes of participation. If participants are falling like flies, it's definitely a good idea to step back when the activity has run its course and figure out how to make the next attempt more satisfying and meaningful to the children.

DIFFERENT STROKES FOR DIFFERENT FOLKS

You'll be thinking a lot about the needs you'd like your cooperative to address. The freedom of creativity inherent in learning cooperatives means they can become anything you want them to be but very broadly, learning cooperatives fall into three categories. To help get your creative juices flowing, let's look at a few existing groups. Use one of these ideas as-is or as a springboard to something that better suits your protégé. You're the coach!

Academic Co-ops

Academic cooperatives tend to focus on specific areas of study. Use your child's report card, and more importantly her input, to figure out your starting point. An academic co-op can provide:

- Remedial Help: Put a new slant on a subject in which your child is having difficulty in order to improve skills and increase interest.

- Advanced Learning: Provides opportunity to dig deeper into a subject in which your child excels.

- Introduction to New Topic—No matter how many subjects are on the school curriculum, it doesn't cover a minute fraction of all the interesting subjects one can study; use this as a way to introduce some of them.

DINE AROUND THE WORLD

"Dine Around the World" is the brainchild of Leslie from Vermont, begun when her only child, Amanda, was seven years-old. "It actually started with just Amanda's Grandma and us," explains Leslie, "taking turns once a month to showcase recipes from around the world. I told a friend about it, she loved the idea so her family joined us, and it took off from there."

Today there are twelve member families with half a dozen or so taking part in each monthly event. "After dinner a family volunteers to be the next host, and after dessert all attendees nominate, then vote on the next month's country," Leslie says. "The host family researches and prepares the menu. They provide the main part of the meal, are in charge of finding out who will attend, and they divide remaining food needs pot luck style."

"In the meantime," Leslie continues, "all the families spend the next month studying the chosen country in any manner they choose. The kids contribute something 'country specific' to the evening. Depending on their ages they might paint a flag, learn and sing a song, or regale us with a popular folk tale. In March, when everyone has cabin fever, we go all out. For this dinner we decorate the dining and living areas in the appropriate motif, and everyone wears ethnic clothing. It's a hoot!"

NOT YOUR ORDINARY BOOK CLUB

Does your child have a favorite series of books? You might take a cue from Patty and Carla's "American Girls Co-op," where eight girls ages seven to twelve gather weekly to share their passion and learn about American history. "It's been five years and we've never come close to running out of related things to do," says Carla. "While there is a lot of merchandise associated with American Girls, for the most part we've focused on the books, which are available through the library, and the magazine, so that no one ever felt they had to spend a ton of money for their daughter to be part of the group."

Next year both of the founders' daughters will be "too old" for the group, but no one is worried. The daughters will "graduate" into new co-coordinators as their moms step down from the roles.

FOREIGN LANGUAGE CO-OPS

To date I've heard of Spanish, French, Latin, Russian, and Japanese co-ops, but with all the languages in the world, I'm sure there are more! Oftentimes schools don't address foreign languages until middle or high school, even though the experts say the best time to learn another language is when we're young. Here's your child's chance.

The clubs use different methods to achieve their goals. Some use the popular computer software, such as Power Glide, Rosetta Stone and, for the really young ones, Muzzy, the cartoon space traveler, on a video series. One meets twice a week and uses a standard textbook for lessons. Once a week another hires a moonlighting school teacher who enjoys the limited class size. Member families of two of the groups hosted foreign exchange students for an immersion experience everyone enjoyed. One group purchases copies of a children's book in the language they study from the Multilingual books Web site. For extra practice, the older children use the site's links to online foreign newspapers.

All the groups use a mix of puzzles and games, lots of visual stimulation, movies, and food to keep the children wanting more. *Pasame el burritos, por favor!*

THE MIX-'EM-UP CO-OP

The idea, says founder of the little group of five, Kate, fits perfectly into her family of six's hectic lifestyle. "We start with a theme," she explains, "then purposely go out of our way to find connections with as many different school subjects as we possibly can."

Her eldest, Joel, is a budding rock star, so they started with music. "That quickly led into math," Kate says, "and branched into the physics of sound, then history. That was so much fun that the kids decided they wanted to do the same thing with astronomy. This was an easy connection to math, and of course we wove in history, art, and mythology literature. If they don't change their minds," she adds, "we're soon moving on to slime science which I'll make sure leads to housekeeping skills, if nothing else!"

THE WRITE STUFF

"Calling all pre-teen Stephen King wannabe's" was the headline of Anne's free classified ad on her city's Web site. She and a friend, a locally published author, thought a writing club where the children could brainstorm, share, constructively criticize, commiserate, and celebrate with other young writers might inspire both of their science-fiction fanatic sons to write a little of their own. "Nine boys and one girl signed on," Anne remembers, "and the girl and three boys made it through to the end of our three-month course. Each finished a short story, and they learned about the submission process at the same time.

"In retrospect we realize the course went on too long, especially since it bridged the change between school and summer schedule. That made it too challenging for the families who have to go into a totally different mode for summer. We were a little too eager to see one of them finish writing a novel," she laughs, "but we learned and toned it down for our next go-round that began in September and only lasted six weeks."

The group is in its third year and has seen many participants come and go, although both of their sons remain committed. "It's one thing to see a complete story in your head," explains Anne, "and quite another to get it down on paper."

The children who stay with it really benefit, she believes. "A couple have gotten short pieces published, but more importantly they walk away a little more confident, a little more sure they can do whatever they put their minds to. When parents call and tell us their children's grades have improved across the board, not just in English, we know it's worth every moment we devote to 'The Write Stuff.'"

Co-ops Based on Interest or Hobbies

Here's where creativity pays big dividends! Brainstorm with your child, let your imaginations soar, and invent a brand new, suit-your-child's-need-to-know, learning cooperative. These co-ops are wonderful for children with:

- Long-held interest—Expands the learning horizon by gathering others with lots of knowledge on a subject.

- Developing interest—Sharpen the learning curve through immersion; you'll be surprised at how rapidly an interested child picks up what she wants to know.

- Need for a deep interest—Experiment with potential topics of interest until the need to learn flame ignites.

COACH'S MOTIVATIONAL MINUTE: We may ask our children what they're interested in, only to hear about comic books, rock music, bugs, or playing in mud. Because it's unlikely that comic books and rock music will appear on a school curriculum, it's hard to think of them as holding any educational value. Hark back to CIAL and remember it's not the topic, but attention that leads to learning. As learning coach you can provide as much time, support,

A recent casual conversation with a new acquaintance revealed that the man's son had risen quickly in the ranks of a computer repair business, was very successful financially, and had been promised by the business' owner that he would take it over when the current owner retires soon. Because I never go off duty from researching, I pressed the man for details of his son's early years. "Oh, yeah!" he exclaimed. "Way back when I bought our first computer (pre-Commodore 64 days) I handled it so gingerly. Then I walked in one day to see he had the whole thing torn apart. I told him, 'You use the keys, you don't take it apart!' and he said he wanted to see what was inside that made it work. He did the same thing to every computer we ever owned."

The man had an "aha!" moment, as this was the very first time he connected that little boy curiosity and interest and ripping apart expensive computer equipment with the successful grown businessman the boy became. "Gee, Linda, I had no idea. Guess I shouldn't have yelled at him, huh?" he concluded.

UNIT STUDIES

Here's a great opportunity to consider what has come to be called unit studies. Start with a child's interest and weave an entire learning tapestry around it, just as Elizabeth did in her home when her son, Sean, now eleven years old, got hooked after watching a popular movie about pirates a few years ago.

"I thought the movie horrid, but after pirates, pirates, pirates for a week and counting," Elizabeth says, "I took it as a challenge to tie it to as many school subjects as possible." First, it was off to the library to find books that Sean could read himself and others Elizabeth read out loud (check off reading and vocabulary). She picked up another pirate movie from the video store to keep the learning fire burning. For a week they spent evenings working on a pirate story. Sean wrote what he could, and dictated more for Elizabeth to write down. When it was done, Sean took another week creating illustrations that turned the story into a book (check off spelling, penmanship, grammar, art).

"I thought the math would be more challenging," says Elizabeth, "but once I got started I couldn't stop, and Sean loved it. I kept throwing out questions like, 'If the captain gave each of his sailors three pieces of eight, and he has nine sailors, how much gold has he passed out?' or 'The pirates need twenty-five barrels of flour before they can set sail, but only eight have been loaded. How many more do they need?'" (check off multiplication and subtraction). By this time Elizabeth had the video store calling her whenever they came across another pirate movie. Sean spent spare time on Internet research and the family took frequent day trips to marinas where Sean spent hours talking with and helping sailboat owners.

The more they learned, the more questions Sean asked. Upon reviewing how successful her plan was when the pirate thing fizzled out after a few months, Elizabeth realized they had also covered:

- How ships are built (Anatomy of ship, experiments involving flotation, buoyancy, displacement)

- Where the pirates came from (Geography)

- What pirates ate (Cooking, health)

- Why men became pirates (Economics, history, ethics)

- Storms (Weather, graphing, measurement)

- Life skills the child became interested in (Astronomy, map reading, knot-tying)

Today Sean takes sailing lessons, has an offer for a job as deck hand when he comes of age, and talks of owning a fleet of charter boats one day, sailing vacationers to the far ends of the earth. Hey, you never know.

POPULAR UNIT STUDIES WITH THE UNDER 12 CROWD

American Girls

The American Girl series (titled American Girls Collection) is a set of stories by a variety of authors told through the eyes of young girls living in different time periods. In addition, book series includes cookbooks (with a "peek" at dining in the past with each character), pastimes of the era, paper dolls, crafts, theater and stationery kits, teachers guides and more. Also includes titles that address body and health care, emotions, friendships, and more. Continuing reinforcement of information via magazine by subscription (http://store.americangirl.com/subscribe) and Web site (americangirl.com) that offers more on the stories, characters, has a fan club and, of course, you can buy the entire line of dolls here, too.

Ancient Egypt

Beginning readers might like Tomie De Paola's *Bill and Pete* (alligators) *Go Down the Nile*, and *Gift of the Nile: An Ancient Egyptian Legend* by Jan M. Mike. For readers seven years and up there are *Mummies Made in Egypt* by Aliki, *Tales of Ancient Egypt* by Roger Lancelyn Green, and *How to Make a Mummy Talk* by James M. Deem. Don't forget David Macaulay's classic *Pyramid* for all. For younger children add Dover Publications' Egyptian costumes paper dolls, the punch-out mummy case, or Dorling Kindersley's *Ultimate Ancient Egypt Sticker Book*. Older students might like the *Ancient Egypt* coloring book by Peter Der Manuelian and the Metropolitan Museum of Art's *Fun with Beads: Ancient Egypt*. Study hieroglyphs and/or make up your own. All would probably enjoy playing Senet (available online or as shareware, as well as a board game version), ancient Egypt's popular board game for more than 3000 years. Do the same with ancient Greece and Rome, too.

Trains (and Boats and Cars and Planes)

Transportation is a great way to study math, geography, history, and much more. Who can resist *The Little Engine that Could* by Watty Piper, or the Thomas the Tank Engine stories? Try also the *Big Book of Trains* by Christine Heap. Top them off with *Ed Emberley's Drawing Book of Trucks and Trains*. For the older child, peruse *The Illustrated Directory of Trains of the World* by Brian Hollingsworth, dive into history with *Freedom Train: The Story of Harriet Tubman* by Dorothy Sterling, or use Peter Riddle's *Tips and Tricks for Toy Train*

Operators to get the most out of your model trains. For board game fun with commerce, try *Empire Builder* or *Rail Baron*. Similar books exist for whatever mode of transportation gets your child's engine running.

Bugs

Lots of good reading in this category. For little ones, try *Anansi the Spider: A Tale from the Ashanti* by Gerald McDermott and *Charlotte's Web* by E. B. White. Children a little older usually enjoy the spider, centipede, glowworm, grasshopper, and earthworm stars of Roald Dahl's *James and the Giant Peach*. Check out insectlore.com for books, models, kits, activity books, games, posters, puzzles, and videos. Web site includes a fun "insectlorpedia." Join the Young Entomol-ogists' Society (http://members.aol.com/ YESbugs/bug club.html). Buy an ant farm. Let that spider spin its web on the front porch and watch how it gets supper. Watch a catepillar's metamorphosis. Dorling Kindersley offers *The Ultimate Bug Sticker Book*. Learn about the cycles of the butterfly with *The Butterfly* board game, and all about bees with *Nectar Collector*.

Calvin and Hobbes

The favorite cartoons are archived all over the Internet—just run a Google search on Calvin and Hobbes. If you prefer to hold a book, gems are collected in such titles by Bill Watterson as *Complete Calvin and Hobbes*, *Indispensable Calvin and Hobbes*, *Lazy Sunday Book*, and *Homicidal Psycho Jungle Cat*.

Computers

Hone in on whether your child is most interested in the mechanics, programming, keyboarding, gaming, or other aspect of computers. If you're the only person in America who doesn't have a family friend or relative who fixes or programs computers, a repair person or local college student would likely spend a bit of time teaching you and your child some basics or answering questions for a reasonable hourly fee. Check out *The Cartoon Guide to the Computer* by Larry Gonick or *A Computer Dictionary for Kids and Their Parents* by Jami Lynn Borman. Younger students can learn about word processing with *Mousetracks: A Kid's Computer Idea Book* by Peggy L. Steinhauser, or use arts and crafts to discover how RAM works in *Kids' Computer Creations* by Carol Sabbeth. Older children can find out how RAM works in *How Computers Work* by Ron White, and learn the lingo with Usborne's *Computer Dictionary for Beginners*.

Dinosaurs

Start with Peter Dodson's *An Alphabet of Dinosaurs*, Miriam Schlein's *Before the Dinosaur*, and the paleontology titles of HarperTrophy's *Let's Read and Find Out Science Series* (which includes *Aliki's Dinosaurs Are Different*) with little folks. Older children might like to read *Dinosaur Dig* by Kathryn Lasky, Dorling Kindersley's *The Visual Dictionary of Dinosaurs,* and *The Science of Jurassic Park and the Lost World* or, *How to Build a Dinosaur* by Rob De Salle and David Lindley. Pump it up with Dover Books' stickers, coloring books, and cut-and-make dinosaur skeleton. Play the *Dinosaurs and Things* and *Dino*

Math Tracks board games, make a diorama, and don't forget to pick up some fossil specimens at your local science store.

Fire Engines, Ambulances, Police Cars

How about an *Official Junior Police Handbook*, with information on detecting strangers and other dangerous (and silly) things from the National Exchange Club? Move on to the *Deputy Fire Marshal Kit* from 888-8-PUEBLO. Young ones can enjoy *Teddy Slater's All Aboard Fire Trucks* and *Tonka: If I Could Drive an Ambulance* by Michael Teitelbaum while an older child learns about *The Fire Station* with Robert Munsch and learns about *The American Ambulance: 1900-2002: An Illustrated History* by Walter M. McCall. Build a model, track down Activision Inc.'s computer game, *Fire Fighter American Heroes*, read books on community helpers, and meet some in your neighborhood by inviting a hungry fire fighter, EMT, or police officer for dinner and conversation, and make sure to visit all the stations.

King Arthur/Robin Hood

Lots of great literature to choose from here. All ages will enjoy Kenneth Grahame's telling of the Saint George story in *The Reluctant Dragon*. Little ones will enjoy *A Medieval Feast* by Aliki, while older children can live the magic through *Adam of the Road* by Elizabeth Janet Gray, *The Black Arrow* by Robert Louis Stevenson, and *The Canterbury Tales* adapted by Geraldine McCaughrean for ages ten and up. Pick up Jim Weiss' audiotape or CD, *King Arthur and His Knights*, and listen while you color Dover Books' King Arthur "stained glass." Don't miss either David MacAulay's book or video called *Castle*, and become a *Castle Explorer* thanks to Dorling Kindersley software. Aspiring knights will enjoy Aristoplay's board game, *Knights and Castles*, and Curiosity Kits includes a booklet on the history of stained glass with its stained glass kit for children ages eight and up.

Little House on the Prairie

Another book series, popular with the approximately elementary to pre-teen females. A "My First Little House Book Series" joined the original for reading to babies and preschoolers. Don't forget non-fiction about Laura Ingalls Wilder, the series' main character, or the variety of associated cookbooks, craft books, and even a guide book in case you'd like to tour the country, visiting the places Laura lived.

Marine Life

Little ones receive an introduction to the vocabulary of the sea in *The Bottom of the Sea* by August Goldin and Thomas Y. Crowell. They might also enjoy *The Magic School Bus on the Ocean Floor* by Joanna Cole and Aliki's *My Visit to the Aquarium*. Most kids can't resist *Exploring the Titanic* with Robert D. Ballard. Classic literature includes *20,000 Leagues Under the Sea* by Jules Verne, *Moby Dick* by Herman Melville, and *Seabird* by Holling C. Holling. Lots of oceanography activities for the 6-12 year age group in Janice Van Cleave's *Oceans for Every Kid*. Dover offers half a dozen coloring books for children ages 8 and up, including *Coral Reef*,

Seashore Life, and *Whales and Dolphins.* The same age group might enjoy PBS' Bill Nye, "the science guy's" 12-experiment book called *Big Blue Ocean. Dreams of Dolphins Dancing* includes a workbook by Joan Bourque. Board game play includes *Ocean Lotto, Save the Whales, Deep Sea Diver;* card game fun with *Krill* or *The game of OCEAN.* Adopt a whale (iwc.org/adopt/adopt.htm), or buy some seashells at nature or science stores.

Robots

Leap into robots via your child's love of Legos; for info check out mindstorms.lego.com. Read about them with 9 year-olds and up in Eyewitness Books *Robot* by Roger Bridgman, the Kingfisher Young Knowledge series title *Robots* by Clive Gifford, and *How to Build a Robot,* also by Clive. Get kits and build your own from places like robotikitsdirect.com or electronictoolbox.com. Check out NASA's Robotics Education Project at robotics.nasa.gov, which includes the "Rep Girl" Program, "a new NASA effort to increase nationwide participation of females students in robotics learning and competitions."

Rocks

Rocks, the study of which is formally known as geology, have been known to jump into children's pockets everywhere, providing lots of opportunity for your child to learn the differences between rocks, gems, minerals, fossils, and meteorites. Faith McNulty's *How to Dig a Hole to the Other Side of the Earth* will entertain the younger crowd, as will *The Magic*

School Bus Inside the Earth by Joanna Cole and *On My Beach There are Many Pebbles* by Leo Lionni. Older kids will find something of interest in Chet Raymo's *The Crust of Our Earth* and the whole family can benefit from the Roadside Geology Series, a collection of state-specific geological information, during trips. How about Ring-of-Fire's activity kits, focusing on mineral identification, with a separate kit for igneous, sedimentary, and metamorphic rocks. Or a volcano kit from Edmund Scientific Co., or a rock tumbler to make your own precious gems? Make your own geode with a kit from ETA (etauniverse.com).

Space

Whether your child is a budding astronomer or astronaut, check out NASA's educational programs at education. nasa.gov/educators.html, or find their reasonably priced videotapes, computer software, kits, and more at core.nasa. gov. Young children can read about the Apollo 11 mission in *Moonwalk: The First Trip to the Moon* and *Stargazers* by Gail Gibbons, a painless introduction to astronomy. For older gazers there are *Postcards from Pluto* by Loreen Leedy, *The Dark Side of the Universe: A Scientist Explores the Mysteries of the Cosmos* by James Trefil, or Nancy Hathaway's *The Friendly Guide to the Universe* (friendly in that it's the entire universe in only 462 pages). Usborne Books offers a pocket-sized *Stars and Planets* book so it's always on hand. Get a star map, study the Zodiac via Greek legends, or perform fun experiments from Robert W. Wood's *Science for Kids: 39 Easy Astronomy Experiments*. Buy and build eight model Space Shuttles that fly from Dover Books, play the *Constellation Station* board game, learn about rockets with Wild Goose Company's *Out to Launch* experiment kit, or paint and assemble the National Geographic Society's 120-piece Solar System puzzle.

SPORTS CO-OPS

With all that remarkable energy churning inside them, it's no wonder sports — and dreams of becoming a super-star — capture the hearts and minds of so many children. And if a sport is what grabs her interest, run with it. If you recall the pressing need for physical exercise discussed in a previous chapter, you'll actually be educationally multi-tasking with a sports co-op!

Across the country, learning co-ops are built around every imaginable sport, both team and individual. In the former, lessons include working with others for the good of all. In the latter, children hone their own skills in a group setting. In both, they work toward becoming their personal best, which boosts self-confidence and esteem. Such results often have an indirect impact on grades and school performance as the life skills of planning, practice, and goal-setting, once learned, are transferred to educational arenas. In every group I contacted, they stressed that winning, while nice, isn't the point.

"Because we're focused on learning," explains Leslie, exemplifying the typical response, "we help the children understand the sport, not just play it." In most cases playing time is matched by time spent learning the history and evolution of the sport, biographies of excellent players and study of what made them so, equipment, rules, safety, and strategy. "No matter how physically gifted a child is,"

Leslie says, "he or she won't become good, let alone great, without this knowledge. It also levels the playing field," she adds, begging forgiveness for the pun, "because it doesn't take long before everyone realizes that the less gifted who play smart catch up quickly."

Due to the popularity of baseball, basketball, football, hockey, and soccer in schools, others often get short shrift. Don't forget to consider the less publicized but equally valuable sports. Check to see what non-school related sports programs your community offers. Keep in mind that while these typically are not as competitive as school programs, the focus is still generally on winning and not education. Some sports co-ops are coached by member parents while others split the cost of hiring a coach either for some basic training or to steadily work with the group.

CHOICE IN SPORTS

• Badminton	• Gymnastics	• Skiing (down
• Bicycling	• Hiking/Climbing	hill and cross
• Boating	• Horseback Riding	country)
• Bowling	• Golf	• Snowboarding
• Boxing	• Ice skating	• Swimming
• Canoeing/	• Lacrosse	and Diving
Kayaking	• Martial Arts	• Tennis
• Cricket	• Paintball	• Track and Field
• Cross Country	• Racquetball	• Volleyball
• Dancing	• Roller	• Waterpolo
• Fencing	skating/blading	• Waterskiing
• Fishing	• Rugby	• Wrestling
	• Skateboarding	

CHESS CO-OP

Adrienne's youngest of four children, Allison, began asking questions about the family's chess set at age five. When she had nothing else to do she'd move the pieces around the board, talking to herself. By the time Allison was nine, not only had she learned to play chess by the rules, no other member of her household was able to present a challenge anymore, and it had been years since her older brothers had beaten her. "So I put a notice up at the library for anyone, any age, interested enough to meet for chess one night a week at our home," says Adrienne. "At first, just one man showed up. I felt a little awkward at first, but he and Adrienne filled the time with talk about the game. I continued advertising on the local access cable channel, and eventually we had about eight people, ages eight to forty-eight, each week. They focused entirely on chess; it was amazing," Adrienne recalls. "The adults were thrilled to be with kids who wanted to learn. After about six months, well, shall we say, it was very noticeable that the kids were winning more and more games."

In December, 2004, Hikaru Nakamura, age sixteen, became the youngest since fourteen year-old Bobby Fisher to be crowned U.S. Chess Champion. "He is tutored at home by his mother," states an Associated Press article. "He said school would take too much time from chess." A learning co-op can provide your child with the time necessary to pursue an interest, just like Hikaru. And who knows, maybe you will also learn a quicker way to checkmate and win.

SOCIAL CO-OPS

Let's face it. Just because we're thrown into a room with ten, twenty, or thirty other people doesn't mean we're having a grand social experience. Our children are no different. Something needs to be the glue that "sticks" human beings together. Sometimes it's personalities that click; other times it's commonalities, or work acquaintances, or interests. Since children don't choose their classmates and, by extension, have no say in the social aspect of their daily environment, enter social co-ops, especially useful for:

- Introverted children—Their interest in the activities, encouraged by seeing that others are interested in the same thing, helps bring them out of themselves.

- Social butterflies—Some people just can't get enough of being around others, and a social co-op increases opportunity to meet and greet.

- The In-betweens—Many children would just like the freedom and opportunity to choose with whom they learn.

LEARNING PARTIES

Is "learning party" an oxymoron? Not at all! There's no rule that says learning must be boring, and nothing will drive home that point like mixing a little education with pleasure.

"We called them parties so kids would want to attend!" says Helen who along with her nine year-old twin sons, Greg and Andy, conceived of the idea a year ago while at the beach near their home. About fifteen boys and girls between nine and fourteen years of age regularly attend the once a week activities. So far they count among their parties skiing, roller skating, ice skating, bowling, swimming, skate boarding, ballroom dancing, collecting shells, kayaking, dolphin watching, basketball, and "once about half the group went to a member family's vacation home in upstate New York for bobsledding," Helen says. "We do our best to speak with someone who really knows the activity before we commence, so it's brief and brilliant lessons prior to jumping into a hands-on experience." Popular parties are repeated.

One week per month is devoted to democratically run organizational tasks, including choosing the next month's activities, and there's time for every member to provide some sort of summary of what he's learned that month. "Basically the sky's the limit," says Helen, "but because they know there's a monthly report to be made they're much attuned to pre-discussing the educational merits of everything. Even the reports are open-ended," Helen continues. "They can turn it into a public speaking gig, or if they prefer they create some sort of demonstration or project. A most popular summary was when two boys teamed up to create a radio personality interviewing a pro bowler. We're getting a lot of radio interviews now."

GETTING TO KNOW YOUR COMMUNITY

Peggy knew Samantha, her then ten year-old daughter, was quiet and withdrawn compared to other children her age. When two years ago she considered the most important aspects a learning cooperative could add to Samantha's life, she focused on social opportunities. Thus began the "Getting to Know Your Community Club."

When after six months it became apparent that the once a week meetings were overwhelming for Samantha, Peggy toned it down to once a month. "That," she says, "was the perfect formula, and Samantha began to look forward to the activities." Each month brought something, or more accurately, someone new into the lives of the half dozen eight to twelve year-old members.

Meetings lasted for two hours, so were held on Friday evenings when the children didn't have to get up for school the next morning. Each month they invited someone from the community whom the children had decided the month before would be interesting to meet. The guest talked with the group for about an hour, and then spent an additional thirty minutes or so relaxing with kids and parents alike while enjoying refreshments. When the guest left, the group spent the next half hour coming to consensus on the top three invitees for the next gathering and assigned someone to make the invitations.

"We've entertained an astronomer, zoo keeper, lapidary artist, state legislator, television star, and," says Peggy, "a bank president who may have become the favorite because he passed out one million dollar bills to all the kids. The parents stay and enjoy the visits as much as the kids. We have a rule that adult questions come last and only if there's enough time. As the children grow more experienced we notice we're talking less and less! Still, the parents gladly fill in when things bog down a bit, too."

When six months ago one member asked, "How come we never go out and meet anybody?" the group transitioned into "every other month mode." Now six times a year they go out for their meetings, either to volunteer at a nursing home, hospital, library, or other organizations in need of some helping hands, or to visit people in their work environment. "While visiting a doctor at the hospital," Peggy remembers, "not only did we get to see my daughter's stomach working via ultrasound, we witnessed the arrival of a Life Flight helicopter. Talk about exciting!"

Learning cooperatives can add a new dimension to your child's life. Whether it's expanding her knowledge of community, diving into academics, kindling new interests or fueling existing ones, a co-op is part of a learning lifestyle sure to increase time together, create lifetime memories of shared activity and, oh, yeah, everyone learns something, too!

TIPS TO MAKE YOUR LIFE EASIER AND YOUR CHILD'S LEARNING COOPERATIVE REWARDING

Gathering groups have glitches—always. Here's a checklist of basics to consider before you start advertising.

- **What?** State the purpose of your group in one sentence. (You'll be able to use this for advertising purposes, too.)
- **Responsibilities?** Will you conduct all meetings? Will you hire someone? Will cooperating parents take turns with meeting and/or other responsibilities?
- **Who?** Who should be in the group? Are adults welcome? Might some children be too young? Based on other answers, do you need to limit the number of participants? (To begin, start off small; you can always grow. In this way participants experience more involvement and receive more individual attention.) Do parents stay and help out, or scoot out the door and return upon completion?
- **When?** How often will the group meet, how long will meet-

ings be, and for how long a period? (To begin, it's recommended that you meet no more frequently than once a week and only for a month or two. This will give you the chance to fix glitches before you go on.) Will activities require additional time spent at home during the week?

- **Where?** Is your home big enough? Do you need to find a no/low cost meeting facility? Could you alternate between the homes of members?
- **Cost?** The first time you guess at cost; the second time you should have a better idea as to the true cost of activities and can more accurately forewarn other parents. Don't forget to factor in costs of tutor and/or meeting facility, if any.

Great journeys begin with one step, and many large and successful learning cooperatives exist today—and have outlasted their creators—because of the early efforts and vision of just a few families. As you enjoy this experience, keep what works, discard what doesn't. And don't be surprised if one day in the not too distant future your child, having watched you set a goal and follow it through, steps up and says, "Hey, Mom, I'm going to start a (fill in the blank) co-op!"

CHAPTER 12

BECOMING AN INFORMED EDUCATION CONSUMER

If today you were in the market for a new car, refrigerator, or the services of a new plumber, chances are you'd take at least a bit of time to research your options. Maybe you'd check on safety features, new innovations, available options, and the best buy for your money. You might surf the Net or pick up a copy of *Consumer Reports* to find out what others who have used a product or service think about it.

Perhaps it's the term "free public school" that often allows us to forget it's a service for which we pay through a collective tax purse into which we regularly invest ever-increasing, goodly sums of money. (Your child is forced, by law, to attend, so it's not free in that respect, either.) Whether you pay for and utilize school service through taxes or directly from your own pocket as a parent of one of the approximately ten percent of children who attend private school, you are a consumer of educational services. Just like the spheres of auto design, appliances, and the latest plumbing gizmo, the world of education is subject to the fad of the month. You need to be informed in order to judge whether jumping on that bandwagon is good for your child. Your child has a very brief time during which to build a firm educational foundation and get the basics right. It would be a shame to have others close this window of opportunity.

STAYING ON TOP OF EDUCATIONAL ISSUES THAT AFFECT YOUR CHILD

"Our schools are . . . factories in which the raw products (children) are to be shaped and fashioned . . . And it is the business of the school to build its pupils according to the specifications laid down."

These words weren't written by some fanatic living in the woods surviving on tree bark. They were penned in 1922 by a man who served as the first dean of the Stanford School for Education, and as a Houghton Mifflin textbook editor, Ellwood P. Cubberly, who intended them to serve as a summary of the goal of public school administration. Many people's ideas and agendas, both past and present, affect your child. As learning coach it's more important than ever for you to know what they are. No matter if your child attends a public or private school, you can't rely on the school's newsletter or an occasional conversation with her teacher. Such information may be tainted with acceptance of the latest education trend, as well as the very human tendency to think that prevalent social problems lie somewhere "out there" but not in our own neighborhoods.

Where once the education of children was a matter of local concern and initiative, that isn't the case today. What happens in your child's classroom is affected by decisions at three levels, and you need to be aware of what's going on at all of them. (This is true whether or not you're a learning coach, so be sure to share this information with any friends or relatives who have children in public school.)

Local

Ask your child's teacher for a copy of the curriculum he or she is following. This outlines the plan of study for the entire year. Call or meet with the teacher to get a handle on the timing and order of the studies so you have some idea of what your child will be studying and when. This way you can think about and plan ahead for learning gym materials you would like to have on hand at the proper time. Using the curriculum as a guide, make a list of things to do, places to go, games to play, and people to speak with about each topic. For example, if your child will be studying the Civil War, and his grandparents live near Gettysburg, with advance notice you could plan a well-timed trip to see Grandma and Grandpa, and add depth, connection, and experience to the study. (And don't forget to invite them on the "field trip"—they'd probably love it.)

Review the curriculum with your child so he, too, has some advance notice of what's in store for the year. Since many curricula are written in "educationese," be sure to translate this into language he can understand. As you review, ask for his thoughts on what might make his studies more interesting and meaningful. This will also help you recognize the topics he's both excited and apprehensive about, more good clues for a learning coach. Begin by enlisting his help on further researching those topics he likes. If he doesn't know how to do this on his own, provide a role model by working alongside him and letting him see and share what you do. He'll probably also be able to suggest books, movies, software, and games of which you're not aware.

Networking with other parents whose children are in the same class as yours gives you an overview of what's happening on a day-to-day basis. Do the same with parents whose children are at the same school but in difference classes, especially those in higher grades your child will soon be in. Ask about teachers, the children's impressions of the teachers, homework load, and topics of study. Scan local media coverage—newspaper, radio, and television—for news about your child's particular school, as well as other schools in the district.

Don't dismiss education news from cities or states other than your own, as trends begun elsewhere often sweep across the country. California and Texas are often the first to come up with ideas that later affect every state. Schools in several states are experiencing success with Individual Education Plans for every student—is yours among them?

Attend as many local school board meetings as you can. They're a great way to get a feel for what's going on, and what the administration is concerned or happy about. In many towns across the country, local access television channels record the meetings, making it easier than ever to stay up to date.

Technology and computer use varies widely among states and even school districts. Is your child's school taking advantage of everything available? What are other schools doing that your school could also? Are there distance learning courses available to your child via computer link-up with other schools?

Don't forget to familiarize yourself with new tests and standards, teacher competence and availability, and information on any special needs your child may have.

Above all, if something doesn't "feel right" about your child's education, don't dismiss your very natural parental instincts. No matter how degreed or well-intentioned any personnel are, you know your child better than all of them. As parent you have every right to question or receive an explanation of any practice. Remember, these folks are concerned with your child only until he reaches the end of compulsory school age, but he is your concern forever.

State

The bulk of decisions about educational issues are made at your state government level. It's wise to befriend and stay in touch with your representatives to learn about changes that are being considered by the education committee, and those that have been forwarded to the legislature for further action. In addition, every state now offers a Web site where, among much other information, you can typically find announcements of new bills, both pending and passed.

While legislators and their aides should be happy to fill you in and answer your questions any time, at election time they're especially eager to meet and greet their constituents. If you've been networking with other parents who are also interested and have questions or concerns, this is a great opportunity to invite any or all of the candidates to meet with you as a group. Again, use your local newspaper, radio, and television news coverage to keep up with stories from your state capitol.

National

While there was a time when public schools were supported by local and state tax dollars, the federal government got into the business of subsidizing them. Each year the percentage of federal support creeps higher. This financial support is typically accompanied by regulation, as is the case with the No Child Left Behind (NCLB) Act. If a state follows the mandates in the Act, it receives a federal subsidy check. If it chooses not to follow, it forgets about the money. The larger the cash flow, the harder it becomes for any state to "just say no."

In March, 2005, the Heritage Foundation reported on the introduction of legislation in Utah by State Representative Margaret Dayton that "would effectively allow Utah to receive federal funding without having to comply with the rules that come with the money. She hopes that 'we won't be jeopardizing our (federal) funding if we don't live the letter of the law.'" Heritage Foundation's report also stated that "Utah's semi-revolt coincides with a new report by the National Conference of State Legislatures (NCSL) that criticizes NCLB's stringent requirements. Hitting hard with 10th Amendment arguments, the NCSL report argues, '[T]his assertion of federal authority into an area historically reserved to the states has had the effect of curtailing additional state innovations and undermining many that had occurred in the past three decades.'"

Your child is affected by NCLB even if she is the one out of ten school-aged children attending private school. The text of the NCLB Act is sprinkled with references to "Participation of Children Enrolled in Private Schools." Here's one example: ". . . a local educational agency shall, after timely and meaningful consultation with appropriate private school officials, provide such children, on an equitable basis, special educational services or other benefits under this part (such as dual enrollment, educational radio and television, computer equipment and materials, other technology, and mobile educational services and equipment) that address their needs, and shall ensure that teachers and families of the children participate, on an equitable basis, in services and activities developed . . ." If taking the money these schools, too, must follow the rules.

You can keep track of the federal hand in education via the news. Watch and listen for the names of your local affiliates of the National Education Association (NEA), American Federation of Teachers (AFT), and Parents Teachers Organization (PTO). One of their primary reasons for existence is to lobby on school issues. When an issue warrants the attention of these organizations or similar ones, it's important to understand its position and why. As your child's learning coach you'll be prepared to judge if that position represents your child's best educational interests.

COACH'S MOTIVATIONAL MINUTE: If you never look up another educational news resource, at least find and read "No Child Left Behind" Final Regulations:

http://www.ed.gov/policy/elsec/leg/esea02/index.html.

It's lengthy, and it's not easy reading. However, it gives you a glimpse of the federal policies currently driving the direction of education in schools, your child's included.

NEWS SOURCES YOU NEED

Just as with your favorite newspaper, magazine, radio, or television program, each of the news sources listed in the sidebar below offers the news from its particular political slant. A couple are rather "in your face" about their reporting, too. If reading a particular source raises your blood pressure to dangerous levels, for heaven's sake, skip it. Hopefully, though, you'll be able to set aside the interwoven political commentary to cull the educational facts conveyed in the reporting, then put your own political spin on them.

While there is no "Education Consumer's Digest" for parents, information sources abound and you'll soon know where to find them. Happy exploring!

NEWS SOURCES YOU NEED

EDUCATION GADFLY: weekly on the Web from Thomas B. Fordham Foundation:
www.edexcellence.net/foundation/global/index.cfm

EDUCATION INFO: randomly received email with information from and about U.S. Department of Education publications. To subscribe, address an email message to: listproc@inet.ed.gov.

EDUCATION INTELLIGENCE AGENCY COMMUNIQUE: weekly email report on teachers'
union activity. Sign up on the Web at www.eiaonline.com

EDUCATION NEWS: daily email with links to actual articles around the globe: www.EducationNews.org

EDUCATION REPORTER: monthly on the Web:
http://www.eagleforum.org/educate/

EDUCATION WEEK: weekly on the Web: www.edweek.org

> **THE E-FILES:** www.e-files.org/
>
> **ED WATCH:** online publication of the Maple River Education
> Coalition: www.edwatch.org
>
> **HERITAGE FOUNDATION EDUCATION NOTEBOOK:**
> www.heritage.org
>
> **SCHOOL NEWS MONITOR:** top ten stories of the week at
> www.eiaonline.com/monitor.htm
>
> **SCHOOL REFORM NEWS:** free subscription at
> www.heartland.org
>
> **TEACHER MAGAZINE:** free email newsletter at
> http://www.teachermagazine.org/

THE LEARNING COACH LEGACY

I leave you with a vision of four valuable gifts you potentially provide your child when you create a learning lifestyle guided by coaching instead of teaching.

First, you encourage your child's autonomy, which is what education and growing up are all about. Earlier I mentioned that the coach perspective transforms your child from a passive recipient of information into an active creator of his education. A natural consequence of this change is the realization that education isn't received—it is achieved. Children blessed with knowledge of this vital truth live and grow with the associated responsibility. Anecdotal evidence strongly suggests that growing and living this way encourage the capacity for autonomy, both educationally and in life in general, relatively early in a child's life compared to many of his peers.

Next, a learning coach focuses on his or her child's personal growth. Growing and living in this way is mentally, emotionally, psychologically, *and* spiritually healthier and saner for a child than growing and living under constant testing and comparison to age-mates. You see, when learning is fun and easy and guided by CIAL, an improved option of assessment automatically becomes available. As learning coach, you are so aware of all the development going on that any indicators of progress you feel you need come directly from your child. Typical academic testing, then, is revealed as a time-consuming, silly, inappropriate burden.

A learning coach gives her child a tailor-made education. Build on his strengths, shore up his weaknesses. Spend more learning time where it's wanted or needed, spend less where it is not. Use the time you free up—and you will free up a remarkable amount—to share real life skills. Or turn the time over to play, a child's land of infinite possibility where curiosity and imagination exercise and grow. When you commit yourself to being your child's learning coach, you allow your child to be a child. Let his interests ignite a firestorm of learning that kindles the next benefit . . .

 . . . the acquisition of basic learning and life skills. Allow your child to follow interests wherever they lead to give CIAL-motivated, hands-on experience in the actual learning process. Yes, that interest may be something with which you're not particularly enamored, but pursuing that interest in depth will at different times require exercising various learning skills including reading, writing, planning and preparing, critical thinking, organizing information, networking, questioning, and so much more. Space, time, and support to discover and exercise these skills through pleasurable pursuits, ideally in a state of flow, is a priceless gift to bestow upon your child, one that when encouraged and nurtured will serve him or her for a lifetime.

So, too, will the life skills you will soon impart as a matter of habit neatly woven into your learning lifestyle. As if to underscore the enormity of this gift, a January, 2005, *Time* cover story by Lev Grossman is titled "They Just Won't Grow Up." The article includes speculation from sociologists, psychologists, and economists as to why the phenomenon of "twixters" (a.k.a. "the boomerang generation"), young adults ages 18-25 who appear to be floundering after college and returning home to live with parents, is growing at such a rapid clip. ("The percentage of twenty-six-year-olds living with their parents has nearly doubled since 1970, from 11 percent to 20 percent, according to Bob Schoeni, a professor of economics and public policy at the University of Michigan.")

It may have much to do with what twenty-seven year-old twixter Matt Swann discovered after six-and-a-half years in college (not terribly unusual anymore—the average student takes five years to finish today) earning a degree in cognitive science, the value of which "in today's job market is not clear." Unable to get a job as a cognitive scientist, Matt took a job waiting tables in Atlanta. "It proved to be a blessing in disguise," writes Lev Grossman. "Swann says he learned more real-world skills working in restaurants than he ever did in school. 'It taught me how to deal with people. What you learn as a waiter is how to treat people fairly, especially when they're in a bad situation.'"

Colleges, the article continues, "are seriously out of step with the real world in getting students ready to become workers in the post-college world. Vocational schools like DeVry and Strayer, which focus on teaching practical skills, are seeing a mini-boom. Their enrollment grew 48 percent from 1996 to 2000."

It's never too early to start keeping an eye on the job market at first, for your child, and then with your child as she becomes capable. Along with learning and life skills you can give her the knowledge she needs to capitalize on her interests and intelligences in a way that will best serve her and her future family's needs. Through conversations about and field trips to places of employment, both those in which she expresses interest and others she doesn't even know exist, you open the world of intelligent possibilities. As learning coach you are uniquely positioned to prepare your child to determine what to do for life's work. (The U.S. government offers an "Occupational Outlook Handbook" at bls.gov/oco/home. htm.)

Finally, please allow me to remind you how truly fortunate you are that first, you're aware enough to know that your family has educational options and second, you're intelligent enough to be researching them. From President Bush's No Child Left Behind Act to its required state testing and accountability, from the push for ever-earlier schooling to the increasing epidemic of "pushing out" less-than-stellar high school students, the outlook for traditional schooling grows bleaker every day.

Your child can rise above this depressing scenario because she has a learning coach at her side. The learning coach approach empowers your family with knowledge you can use to build a worthwhile education together. It offers hope for struggling children, a challenge for bored ones, and meaning for all. The learning coach approach supplies a map for your educational journey—you need only add the love, encouragement, support, and smiles.

CONGRATULATIONS

Congratulations. You are now a learning coach. You have at your disposal the freedom to guide your child's education through your heart, with love. Over the years I've seen the positive results of this freedom repeated often enough to know this makes all the difference in the world. Guiding with love allows you to replace the authoritarian hierarchy of teacher/student with the reciprocity and mutual respect that grow in friendship. It keeps you as parent humble, gentle, and honest. It gives you energy, patience, and strength. Yes, embracing this freedom will transform your child's educational experience, but it will also transform your relationship with your child and, trust me, it will transform you as an individual, too.

It is my hope that becoming a learning coach during your child's remarkable journey toward adulthood makes it just as fun and interesting and informative and exciting and educational and as filled with love and togetherness as was my experience with my children —once I finally woke up. The experience is far too short, so let the learning coach approach make it just as sweet as it can be.

Thank you for reading this book. May the learning road rise up to meet you and yours.

APPENDIX A

READING TO LEARN MORE

Armstrong, Thomas, Ph.D. *In Their Own Way: Discovering and Encouraging Your Child's Personal Learning Style.* Jeremy P. Tarcher, 1987.

Armstrong, Thomas, Ph.D. *Awakening Your Child's Natural Genius: Enhancing Curiosity, Creativity, and Learning Ability.* Jeremy P. Tarcher, 1991.

Barfield, Linda. *Real-Life Homeschooling: The Stories of 21 Families Who Make It Work.* Simon and Shuster, 2002.

Brown, Ken. *The Right to Learn: Alternatives for a Learning Society.* Routledge Press, 2002.

Brainerd, Lee Wherry, et. al. *Basic Skills for Homeschooling: Language Arts and Math for the Middle Years.* Learning Express, 2002.

Bruinsma, Sheryl. *Look Before You Leap and Other Lessons for Kids.* Baker Publishing Group. 2001.

Buckingham, David and Scanlon, Margaret. *Education, Entertainment and Learning in the Home.* McGraw-Hill, 2003.

Cheatum, Billye and Hammond, Allison A. *Physical Activities for Improving Children's Learning and Behavior: A Guide to Sensory Motor Development.* Human Kinetics Press, 2000.

Crain, William. *Reclaiming Childhood: Letting Children Be Children in Our Achievement-Oriented Society.* Owl Books, 2004.

Czikszentmihalyi, Mihaly. *Finding Flow: The Psychology of Engagement with Everyday Life.* Basic Books, 1998.

Diamond, Marian, Ph.D. and Janet Hopson. *Magic Trees of the Mind: How to*

Nurture Your Child's Intelligence, Creativity, and Healthy Emotions from Birth through Adolescence. Plume Books, 1999.

Dickinson David, Tabors, Patton. *Beginning Literacy with Language: Young Children Learning at Home and School.* Paul H. Brookes Publishing Company, 2003.

Dobson, Linda. *The Art of Education: Reclaiming Your Family, Community and Self.* Holt associates, 1997.

Dobson, Linda (Ed). *The Homeschool Book of Answers: The 88 Most Important Questions Answered by Homeschooling's Most Respected Voices.* Prima Publications, 1998.

Dobson, Linda. *Homeschooling the Early Years: Your Complete Guide to Successfully Homeschooling the 3 to 8-Year-Old Child.* Random House, 1999.

Dobson. Linda. *The First Year of Homeschooling Your Child: Your Complete Guide to Getting Off to the Right Start.* Prima Publishing, 2001.

Dobson, Linda. *The Ultimate Book of Homeschooling Ideas: 500 + Fun and Creative Learning Activities for Kids Ages 3–12.* Prima Publishing, 2002.

Dobson, Linda. *What the Rest of Us Can Learn from Homeschooling.* Random House, 2003.

Elkind, David, Ph.D. *The Hurried Child: Growing Up Too Fast Too Soon.* Perseus Books, 2001.

Faber, Adele and Mazlish, Elaine. *How to Talk So Kids Will Listen So Kids Will Talk.* Perennial Currents Publishing Co., 1999.

Faber, Adele and Mazlish, Elaine. *Liberated Parents, Liberated children: Your Guide to a Happier Family.* Avon Books, 1990.

Gatto, John., Dumbing Us Down: *The Hidden Curriculum for Compulsory School.* New Society Publishing, 2002.

Healy, Jane M., Ph.D. *Endangered Minds: Why Children Don't Think and What*

We Can Do about It. Touchstone, 1990.

Hirsh-Pasek, Kathy, et.al. *Einstein Never Used Flash Cards: How Our Children Really Learn—And Why They Need to Play More and Memorize Less*. Rodale Books, 2003.

Holt, John. *Learning All the Time*. Addison Wesley Publishing, 1990.

Jirak, Mary Ellen. *The Gift of ADD: Shattering Labels and Changing Expectations for Parents and Teachers*. (gr8beginnings.com)

Kochenderfer, Rebecca and Kanna, Elizabeth. *Homeschooling for Success: How Parents Can Create a Superior Education for the Children*. Warner Books, 2002.

Layne, Marty. Learning at Home: *A Mother's Guide to Homeschooling*. Sea Change Publshing, 2000.

Ledson, Sidney. *Teach Your Child to Read in Just Ten Minutes a Day*. Trafford Press, 2004.

Levine, Mel. *A Mind at a Time: America's Top Learning Expert Shows How Every Child Can Succeed*. Simon & Schuster, 2003.

Liewellyn, Grace and Amy Silver. Guerrilla Learning: *How to Give Your Kids a Real Education With or Without School*. J. Wiley and Sons, 2001.

Morgan, Melissa and Waite, Judith. *Homeschooling on a Shoestring: A Jam-Packed Guide*. Waterbrook Publishers, 1999.

Schmidt, Laurel. *Seven Times Smarter: 50 Activities, Games, and Projects to Develop the Seven Intelligences of Your Child*. Three Rivers Press, 2001.

Willis, Mariaemma and Victoria Kindle Hodson. *Discover Your Child's Learning Style: The Key to Every Child's Learning Success*. Prima Publishing, 1999.

APPENDIX B

WEB SITES AND OTHER RESOURCES

Reading for You

All Kinds of Minds: allkindsofminds.com

Best Homeschooling: besthomeschooling.org (you won't *believe* the resources you'll find at this excellent site)

Brain Connection Brain Buzz: brainconnection.com

Freedom in Education: freedom-in-education.co.uk

GenieU: A Safe Haven for Your Child's Genius: genieu.com

How No Child Left Behind Undermines Quality and Equity in Education: fairtest.org/Failing_Our_Children_Report.html

Learning Style Test:
http://parentcenter.babycenter.com/calculators/learningstyle/learningstyle1jhtml

Parent Educator: theparenteducator.com

Worksheet Sources: http://sitesforteachers.com/index.html, http://teachers.teach-nology.com/index.html

TYPICAL CURRICULUM

Developing Educational Standards: Edstandards.org/standards.html

Kids Connection: Kidsconn.com/first.html

REVIEWS AND RECOMMENDATIONS FOR CHILDREN'S LITERATURE

American Library Association: http://ala.org

Books About Pets: http://www.hsmo.org/education/readlist.html

Children's Literature Web Guide: http://www.ucalgary.ca/-dkbrown

Cynthia Leitich Smith Children's Literature Resources: http://www.cynthialeitichsmith.com/index1.htm

Eager Readers: http://www.eagerreaders.com

Hoagie's Kids and Teens: http://www.hoagieskids.org

International Children's Digital Library: http://www.icdlbooks.org

MAGAZINES

Home Education Magazine—bi-monthly: homeedmag.com

Life Learning: LifeLearningMagazine.com

Paths of Learning: pathsoflearning.org

BRAIN-BASED LEARNING

funderstanding.com/brain_based_learning.cfm

members.shaw.ca/priscillatheroux/brain.html

Resources

Aristoplay: aristoplay.com

Ball-Stick-Bird learn-to-read books: ballstickbird.com

Bi-Linqual Books: bbks.com

Bits & Pieces: bitsandpieces.com

Family Math Jean Kerr Stenmark, et. al. (University of California, Berkeley, Lawrence; 18th edition, 1976)

FUN Books: fun-books.com

Greathall Productions: greathall.com

Mindware: mindwareonline.com

Muzzy, the BBC Language Course for Children: early-advantage.com
Power Glide (foreign languages): power-glide.com

President's Council on Physical Fitness and Sports: fitness.gov

Rosetta Stone (foreign languages): rosettastone.com

Two good, inclusive books for general, all-purpose use:

The Home School Source Book by Jean and Donn Reed

The Complete Home Learning Source Book: The Essential Resource Guide for Homeschoolers, Parents, and Educators Covering Every Subject from Arithmetic to Zoology by Rebecca Rupp

For Your Learning Team

WEB SITES

Astronomy: kidsastronomy.com

Awesome Library: awesomelibrary.org

Chem Comics: uky.edu/Projects/Chemcomics

Daily math and reading exercises for elementary-aged kids: beestar. org/index.jsp

eCyberMission Competition: ecybermission.com (Army-sponsored science, math, and technology competition for students grades 6-9)

International Children's Digital Library: icdlbooks.org

Journaling Life: journalinglife.com

Kids' Business: kids4kids.biz (encourages children to begin their own businesses and provides the tools they need to do so)

Math and Science for You: MathAndScience4U.com—weekly newsletter via email; daily problem-solving activity on Web site

Newspapers of the World: newspaperlinks.com

New Scientist: weekly e-newsletter; newscientist.com

Our Planet: emagazine.com (environmental news delivered by email)

Power Politics III Game (free): csmonitor.com/specials/decision2004/power-politics/index.html

GAMES TO IMPROVE SPELLING/VOCABULARY SKILLS

Boggle, Jr.

Scrabble, Jr.

Pictionary, Jr.

Taboo, Jr.

Smart Mouth

Hangman

A to Z, Jr.

Tri-Bond, Jr.

Double Quick

Syzgy

Upwords

Scattergories, Jr.

Jumble

Quick Word

Outburst, Jr.

Perquackey

Quble

My Word, Jr.

Blurt

Quiddler

GAMES TO IMPROVE MATH SKILLS

Rook

Uno

Hearts

Lucky 13

Racko

Dominos

Sequence for Kids

TriOminos

Tripoley

'Smath

Make 7

Stock Market Tycoon

Arithmetrix

Mixmath

Moneywise Kids

Flinch

Battle Dot

24

APPENDIX C

ACTIVITIES FOR LEARNING FUN AT HOME

It's So Nice to Have Some Numbers Around the House

Let your child experiment with measures and temperatures to make cookies and take and learn from mistakes when he messes up—he will soon see that two cups means just that.

A cheap calculator has some numerical games on it—play them with your child.

Let her buy a penny stock—and show her how to track it in the stock market quotes.

Open up a checking account for your child—put $500 in it for college. Let her write a few checks up to $10.00 (if anyone will take the check). Let her reconcile the account and get a little mail. Show her what interest is.

Adopt a child somewhere in the world by contributing a few dollars which your child can earn with some very select family chores. Let him send the money in and see how far a few dollars goes in another country to buy rice (and how far it does not go in this country).

Teach her the value of a dollar against a Canadian dollar, a Euro, and yen. Let her graph it on a weekly basis.

Have your child create an inventory of household furniture and important things (for insurance purposes, for example). Have him count how may books, T.V.'s, dishes, plates, glasses, etc. Explain to him why this is necessary (in case of fire, hurricane or tornado it can help).

Put your child on a scale; put everyone on a scale. Have your child chart everyone's weight over the next year. How much does the dog weigh? How much does the cat weigh? (For an easier graph, have younger children graph all relatives' ages.)

Learn fractions by helping with dinner. "Sweetie, I need half of a potato, a cup of water, a teaspoon of sugar, 1/4 of an apple."

Put a height marker on a back out-of-the-way wall someplace. Mark it off (or have your child do so) in feet and inches. Mark it every six months with your growing child's height. He will soon understand feet, inches, and how children grow relative to time.

How many pages does the paper have on Monday vs. on Sunday. On the average? What is an average?

Next time you take a trip, take out a map and show your child the map's scale of miles and direction. Work with him to determine how far you are going to go in miles. In which direction?

Explain the car's odometer and the gas gauge—and how many miles per gallon the car gets. See if he can help figure out where the gas gauge will wind up when you get to Grandma's for Thanksgiving.

Make a project out of tracking the cost of gasoline for a year.

Give your child an idea of what things cost, and what the household budget is . . . and whether or not something can be afforded and why.

Decimals? They scare everyone. Show your child—in simple terms—what it might cost them in interest to borrow money for a fancy bike (at a low interest rate and a high interest rate). Discuss what the decimal means.

Give her some type of allowance with which to budget. This will help her learn what savings are and how to plan to purchase or acquire something she wants.

Teach her about calories . . . how many does a growing child need? Show him the calorie count in the food he is eating. Have him set up a calorie budget. Who knows, maybe he'll tell *you* that he shouldn't eat the whole box of chocolate chip cookies.

Never underestimate the power of a simple game of marbles for a youngster who might want to count "marble" earnings. Dad, can you even remember how to play marbles?

Come up with a variety of activities that requires your child to watch the clock and determine when an activity shall begin. Your child wants to go to the beach? "Ok, honey, we will go at 11:15 this morning." She will soon figure out when 11:15 is.

Help your child learn about time zones and why it's three hours later in California than in New York.

At what rate do we use paper towels in the house? So how much should we have on hand? When should we buy more? Put your child in charge of counting and "ordering" paper towels. She'll find out very soon from the rest of the family why this "simple" job needs to be done well.

Pick a relative in a different area of the U.S., maybe where it is very hot or very cold, and have your child keep a log of the temperatures over a year. This will require you to give the child a basic awareness of temperatures and what a thermometer is.

Got Hurricanes? Even if you don't, help your child gain a basic understanding of what is means when we say that the wind is blowing at a certain speed and what wind can do to a home or town when it exceeds certain speeds. All areas are prone to windstorms; what speed means danger?

As soon as your child receives a math textbook at school, you, as learning coach, can familiarize yourself with its contents and be prepared to take the mystery out of the math. Textbooks often are not written well, and your gentle and guiding interpretation of a confusing presentation may make the difference between your child "getting it" and not getting or understanding the math being presented.

Put an inexpensive rain gauge outside. Have your child keep a log of the amount of rain over a period of time; she'll develop an understanding of what it means when the weather man says that was "five inches of rain."

Put a wind speed indicator on the roof of the house with a gauge in the living room so your child can associate wind speed with different types of weather.

Give your child a 20 foot tape measure. Go around with him and measure things—the car, how tall his older brother is, the width of the driveway, how tall he is, how long the cat is. It is amazing how much he'll learn about life this way.

Spell Check

When you are planning to go on a long trip on an expressway, obtain, in advance, a large print map or atlas and circle key cities, exits, and sites you'll be passing. While on the trip, have your youngster identify them as you pass exit signs and billboards identifying cities and towns, etc. Pronounce the name of the city or town for the child and play with the spellings.

Depending on where you live (and the time of the year)—and if you are on an expressway—you may see a lot of license plates from out of state. Create a checklist of all of the states in the US. Have your child look for those license plates on those long boring trips. When he sees New York or Florida on a license plate and can match that with the list you have given him, have them put a big check mark next to the state name. Pronounce the name for him and have him spell it out loud. Repeat this on the next trip using the same list. It won't be long before he can spell and even recite most, if not all, of the states of the Union. Later in life that will come in handy when he hits the road on his own.

Hopefully your child has a collection of toys somewhere in a box or a bin. On a rainy day when she is playing with the bin's contents, pick out the toys one by one and have her write out (or you write it out) on a sheet of colored paper what the name of the toy is and its spelling. Have the child pronounce and spell the name. This gets old after a while, but it is fun in the beginning—especially if Mom is working with her at it.

You're not always on an expressway, but around towns there is no lack of green and red lights, stop signs, "hazard," "school," "slow," "caution," "bridge is icy when wet," etc. Make a list of such signs that your child can look for and identify and check off. Use the same pronunciation and spelling techniques as outlined above. It won't be long before she knows each and every traffic sign in your town! Won't hurt when that driver's test comes along all too soon!

Certainly your child has some favorite things he does, certain friends or pets he likes, parts of the house or neighborhood to which he enjoys going, etc. Work with him to identify who or what or where these people or things are. List them on a sheet of paper, pronounce the word, and help your child spell it. Because it is a favorite friend, or place, or pet, he'll be more inclined to want to learn to say and spell it just like an adult.

Walk down a street together, watch for car license plates, billboards, and advertisements, and work through the alphabet progressively one letter at a time in "competition" with your child. Work from A to Z, e.g.: "Oh, I see a sign that says apple, therefore I have the 'A' and then spell 'apple.'" And maybe your child finds a sign that says "fable" and says, "I got the 'B' in fable; 'f-a-B-l-e,'" and so on until the first one gets to Z and wins.

All T.V.'s now have closed-captioning. As your child sees a "dog" on T.V. point out the spelling of "dog." A wonderful way to learn spelling and language.

Learn American Sign Language (ASL) with your child so you can finger spell as she learns the alphabet. A wonderful and fun way to do the ABC's, but it's also a neat "secret language" in which "only you" communicate—at least in your family and maybe the neighborhood. This basic sign language may be helpful as a second language when your child gets to college or later in life if she works with a hearing impaired/deaf person.

Get comfortable with your child with some poster board, glue, and words or letters cut out from ads that are colorful. Create a picture of a Christmas tree or something else with colored words, and spell and learn those words. Your child can also use cut-out words from magazines to send you amusing notes like, "Mom, I want turkey and I want it now!"

Food is a great motivator. Give your child the feeling that you might be quite responsive if he spells "cookie" or "cake" or "pie," rather than just saying it. Ask him to say it and spell it. "Mom, can I have a c-o-o-k-i-e?" "Mom, what's for s-u-p-p-e-r?"

Teach your child how to play a basic word game such as Scrabble. Perhaps Dad and your child team up against Mom for a game, and Dad can help the child play. When your child is a little better and can play on her own, let her have a dictionary to look up words. Children are naturally competitive with their parents, and sooner or later you'll be beat fair and square (dictionary or not).

Fill an empty can with words that relate to things that your child likes, knows, wants, needs, is interested in, etc. Maybe just after dinner, shake the can up, pick a word, and have everyone at the table practice spelling it. Not just your child, everyone. (He needs to know this is a family thing.) The same can can be used for certain jobs around the house or games to play. Your child sees the words and spells them out: "OK, guess I am going to help b-r-u-s-h the c-a-t."

Spelling and the pronunciation of words go hand in hand. (Many of the above games should also encourage a child to pronounce a word correctly.) Help your child learn the proper sound of a letter of the alphabet, then have him create a collection of pictures of items that begin with that sound.

When you want to tell your child something very important, or express to him that he has done something very well, or that you love her very much, tell her with a written note on a piece of nice stationery. Since this nice note is from "Mommy to me"—she's going to want to understand it. Go over the note to show the spelling, phonetics, and meaning of words you use. Purposely use more and more difficult words to heighten their awareness of spelling. Encourage other family members to write to the child and go over that note or letter with her. Bring the notes out a few days later and ask her about the spelling she's learned and to help her remember with hints.

Help your child to find a friend somewhere in the world with whom she can communicate in writing. Pen pal or e-pal, your child will *love* getting mail from abroad and will be eager to sit down with you as a learning coach and parent to see what is being said by the new friend. Help explain new words to the child. Ask her to spell the words and pronounce them.

Make a list with your child of homonyms, English words that sound the same but may be spelled differently: e.g. deer and dear; rein and rain; bear and bare; and so on. Make a game out of it with other family members to see who can get the most combinations.

As learning coach, continually follow-up with your child about the spelling and meaning of new words. These learning activities need to be reinforced and repeated over time; it's not a one shot deal. Your child isn't going to remember the spelling of a word with just one exposure—there needs to be repetition and reinforcement in a fun and positive way.

Science

Take your child to the public water supply station and show her the works and pumps.

Give your child an inexpensive scrapbook, camera, and book on birds of your area. Enjoy "hunting" and "capturing" the birds together with the camera. Make a project of mounting the pictures with time and date.

Identify the trees in your backyard, neighborhood, and community.

On a clear night, grab a star chart and learn together to identify the constellations. Knowledge of the location of the North Star could save a life one day.

Stay up and watch the eclipse together.

Visit a farm or local market of some type. Most any farmer will take ten minutes to show the barn to you and your child.

Take your child to the airport and explain about how planes fly. Science lesson at the same time you minimize her fear of flying.

There's a lot to see at an Army, Coast Guard, or Air Force base.

Buy some flower or vegetable seeds. Plant a bulb in the winter. She may grow up to love plants and flowers when she creates a living thing.

Pick up an inexpensive microscope at a garage sale and look into the world of the infinitesimal.

Pick up a telescope and look into the world beyond.

Build a birdhouse—they'll come! Make a hummingbird feeder out of a plastic water bottle.

Personal Safety

Making a snow fort or simply burying yourselves in the snow teaches your child how warm snow is in an emergency.

Get a guide to edible plants in your region and take a "field" trip in your back-yard or around the corner. Find the plants, bring them home, and eat them. It teaches survival.

Show your child how to take a tin can, put a candle in it, and fry an egg; she may need to some day.

Build a survival fire in the rain then cook on it.

Put your child "in charge" of maintaining emergency flashlights, water, food, and other things for the house and car depending on where you live.

Visit your local fire station or rescue squad. Barring a crisis, firemen and Emergency Medical Technicians (EMTs) would happily speak with your family and show you around. Who knows; maybe even get a ride in the fire engine! Follow up with talk at home about fire safety.

Buy a fire extinguisher; show your child how it works, then put out a small fire with it together.

Perform a family fire drill. Let your child run it and be the pretend Fire Marshall.

Prepare a fire evacuation plan together.

Let her pump gas into the car (under your watchful eye). Use the time to tell her all about gasoline.

Life Skills

Show how your well, well pump, and pressure tank work.

Take your child to a hospital or a nursing home; let him see what there is to see. Talk with the elderly and let your child experience the feeling of bringing happiness to an old, lonely person.

Help your child collect money and account for it for a charity.

Chess—the game of kings. Teach your child how to play, then make one move a day or a week. No rush.

Use the bathtub for a few lessons in rotary breathing, the basis for all good swimming.

Take a taxi, subway, train, or bus ride to some unknown part of the city or town. Help your child get comfortable with and learn to use these modes of transportation she might need some day.

Learn to read music together. Julliard next?

Make a small "violin" or "guitar." Elvis?

Bake a loaf of bread or a bunch of cookies.

Explain recycling. Maybe there's a way you can do it even if your town doesn't. Show your child how to redeem soda cans for money, and help him do so.

Adopt a highway with your child and perform regular clean-ups. Great chance to explain how you are helping the environment and animals.